WHITETAIL
MONARCHS

WHITETAIL MONARCHS

LEGENDS OF AUTUMN

TEXT AND PHOTOGRAPHY BY
GEORGE BARNETT

WILLOW CREEK PRESS

MINOCQUA, WISCONSIN

Published by Willow Creek Press
P.O. Box 147, Minocqua, Wisconsin 54548

For information on other Willow Creek titles,
call 1-800-850-9453

Edited by Greg Linder
Designed by Patricia Bickner Linder

Library of Congress Cataloging-in-Publication Data

Barnett, George
    Whitetail monarchs : legends of autumn / text and
photography by George Barnett.
        p.   cm.
    Includes bibliographical references
    ISBN 1-57223-267-6
    1. White-tailed deer.   2. White-tailed deer Pictorial
works.   I. Title.
    QL737.U55B3635   1999
    599.65'2—dc21   99-38315
                                                          CIP

Printed in The United Kingdom.

CONTENTS

ACKNOWLEDGMENTS

I have many people to thank for the beautiful images of the animals featured in this work. This book represents twelve years of travel and photography across many states where big whitetails are known to roam. My work brought me into contact with people from many different walks of life, and each of their contributions was significant.

Gerald, Mark and Monty Ryals of Wild Country Whitetails
Jim Bevins and Larry Barger from the Genetic Whitetail Research Institute
Jack Reneau and Julie Tripp from the Boone and Crockett Club
Thanks also to:
Jerry Smith for his encouragement during the early years, and Billy Powell,
Randy Meador, Steve Hammack, George and Elizabeth Jambers, Gene Gonzales,
Glenn Sodd, James Robison, Russell Thornberry, Louie Schreiner,
Gordon Whittington, Don Keller, Ray Sassar, Bob Threlkeld, Ray Petrie,
Dan Bouge, Bryan Murphy, Robert Williams, Jim Ballard, Greg Pierson,
Bob Bierstedt, Bill Martindale, Steve Cox, Dr. Jerry Cotner, Ray Murski,
Jim Raney, Nikki Morgan, Wayne Pederson, Terry Sablatura,
Brett Holcomb, Dink Benton and the staff of the
Hagerman National Wildlife Refuge.
Thanks also to Greg and Pat Linder whose input and assistance were
critical to the completion of *Whitetail Monarchs: Legends of Autumn.*

DEDICATION

This book is dedicated to my family, Adelfa, Clayton, and Jessica.
Thanks for all of the support and the many sacrifices. I love you all.
It is also dedicated to my father, who had the foresight to
introduce me to the pleasures of the outdoors at a very young age.
Thanks, Dad.

INTRODUCTION

I remember vividly, as if it were only yesterday, my first encounter with a whitetail deer. It was an event of no great worldly consequence; however, the episode made an impression, to say the least. I was a very young boy of four on that wonderful autumn morning, playing in the yard of some family friends who lived on the edge of the small country town where my father coached the high school football team. An old car pulled into the front yard, and a man dressed in overalls ran anxiously to the front door. Soon all of the men present, including my father, were hurrying to the car as if it were Christmas morning and some great gift waited under the Christmas tree. The trunk of the car was opened. Inside lay a magnificent whitetail buck, recently harvested by the lucky hunter.

As the men admired this fallen monarch, they listened intently as the hunter recounted over and over the details of his successful hunt, unaware of the young boy straining for a glimpse of whatever was causing all of the excitement. I finally squeezed between my father and the hunter and climbed onto the fender of the old car. I sat on the edge next to the fallen giant's head and stared in awe at the old buck's antlers. I ran my hands over the long tines and sweeping beams that were heavy with mass and the color of stained mahogany. Again and again, I counted the points—thirteen in all. I had never seen such an animal; at the time, they were very rare in North Texas. When the time came for the hunter to leave and the trunk to be closed, I would have nothing to do with it. I remember my father prying my hands loose from the buck's antlers as I kicked and screamed to no avail, begging to count the tines and touch the prized trophy one additional time.

I am sure that no one present on that day realized the magnitude of the event in my mind. It is impossible to comprehend how a relatively obscure event could leave such an indelible mark on a small child's mind. However, from that day on, anytime we drove into the surrounding countryside, my gaze remained fixed out the window, scanning the meadows and woods for a glimpse of one of these great animals, but to no avail. The whitetail deer remained a rarity, and sightings were few and far between.

My search was placed on hold a few years later, when a move to the West Coast all but eliminated the chances of seeing my first whitetail buck in the wild. I spent the next ten years dreaming of the great buck in the back of the old car, and what it might have looked like on that fateful morning for the hunter as the buck appeared like a ghost from the shadows of the early morning light.

I spent long hours allowing my vivid imagination to run wild, creating one scenario after another. The mental process of creating an image of the event in my mind was obviously a formative one in my eventual development as a wildlife photographer. I spent afternoons at magazine counters, poring over nature and hunting magazines. I studied the images that appeared on their pages, reading and learning all that I could about this wonderful creature. Although other kids idolized rock stars and football players, my idol was Jerry Smith, perhaps the best whitetail deer photographer to ever carry a camera into the field. Through a chance meeting later in life, Jerry became extremely influential in my decision to pursue this profession.

Whitetail Monarchs

On a cold December morning in 1986, this magnificent whitetail buck appeared from the shadows of a tiny refuge in North Texas, and became the first of many great bucks photographed by the author. The buck gained national attention years later as the legendary "Mr. Big," one of the largest bucks ever photographed in the wild.

As a teenager I lived in Oklahoma, where I further honed my fascination with whitetail deer. Efforts to restock the whitetail in habitats that had not seen the species for decades had been successfully completed around my hometown. Though they were still sparse at best, deer were occasionally sighted around the countryside, and each sighting created a great deal of excitement within the community.

I spent every spare hour in the field hunting with my father, usually for quail and dove. However, the intrigue and allure of the whitetail buck haunted me, calling me to the dense woods not far from my grandparents' house on the Cimarron River. There lived an elusive giant—a great non-typical with over twenty points and massive main beams that was pursued to no avail by every hunter in town. Like most mature dominant bucks, he died from old age, frustrating all who yearned to call his magnificent antlers their own.

Every year, the arrival of autumn fueled a fire deep within my soul. I envisioned one day crossing paths with this majestic

Racing for the safety of cover, this big Hagerman buck offered only a fleeting opportunity for the recording of an image. Seldom is there a second chance to record a great image of a monster whitetail buck.

creature and fantasized about what it might be like to capture one of these giants on film for the entire world to behold. In the fall of 1986, I realized my dream on a small wildlife refuge in North Texas known as the Hagerman National Wildlife Refuge. A duck and goose wintering area, the Hagerman was virtually unknown as a haven for whitetail deer at that time. However, I soon discovered this refuge contained bucks like no other place on earth. I dare say that there were more Boone and Crockett bucks per square mile on the Hagerman than on any other place in the country, including the best private game ranches. The bucks were not your typical small-bodied *texanus* subspecies, either. These were enormous bucks with massive antlers typically seen on the Dakota or *borealis* subspecies. Many local sources indicate that Hagerman's bucks actually were these subspecies, transplanted to the area over fifty years ago on a ranch site now covered by Lake Texoma.

Photographing whitetail deer on the Hagerman Refuge was an educational adventure like no other I have ever experienced. I developed a deep respect and appreciation for the whitetails' cunning ability, their wariness, and their capacity to appear and fade into nothingness at the blink of an eye. I also learned firsthand the positive effects of healthy herd dynamics, including balanced sex ratios, age structure, and population numbers well within the carrying capacity of the land. The role of the predator was also allowed to play out uninterrupted by the human hand, with positive results for the entire herd. The bucks of the Hagerman ate well, grew old, and developed into kings of the autumn woods.

As a photographer, I learned that long hours, quick thinking, and immediate action were essential ingredients to success. Seldom was there a second opportunity to record a great image. Persistence and patience became the virtues of this trade. The hours spent sitting and waiting were many; the rewards, though gratifying, were few and far between.

During one season on the Hagerman, I pursued an enormous buck that I nicknamed "Mr. Big" for more than ten weeks before obtaining my first photograph of the animal. I will never forget the instant this great monarch emerged from the forest and stood before me. I had been fortunate to obtain a few photographs of the buck the year before, but I was not prepared for the sight he presented that unforgettable evening. With massive main beams, thirty-four non-typical points, drop tines, and body mass over three hundred pounds, his appearance on the field signaled to all other deer that he was the king of his domain. As the buck stood statuesque less than thirty yards in front of me, it was several moments before I could catch my breath. I was sure he could hear my heart pounding in my chest, and I feared that the sound would surely belie my position.

From that moment on, I formed a relationship of sorts with the buck, and he offered over a dozen opportunities for photographs over the next two-month period. He apparently became as curious about me as I was fascinated with him, often standing in the open field staring at me as I frantically and clumsily tried to record his image on film. On several occasions, the old buck appeared behind me within a few yards of my ground blind, nearly bringing about heart failure when I turned and made eye contact. Though I was rather unskilled with the camera at the time and my equipment was not what it is today, I did manage a few respectable images of the deer, and he secured for me my first national cover in 1988. I never had an opportunity to photograph Mr. Big under optimal conditions, and today I still dream of how some of those images might have appeared had there been just a little sunlight.

I photographed many other bucks on

The 1987 version of Mr. Big was a spectacular sight to see. On this overcast morning, I caught the old monarch crossing the road headed back into his favored bedding area in the bottomlands of the Hagerman Refuge.

the Hagerman, but none as impressive as Mr. Big. I saw bigger bucks—much bigger. I was just not as lucky the second time around. I still visit the Hagerman from time to time; however, these great monarchs are not as plentiful as they were a decade ago. I am fortunate to have photographed thousands of deer since that unforgettable evening; some that have made me catch my breath, some that have resurrected the memories of my youth, and a few even bigger than Mr. Big. However, I will never forget the evening I first laid eyes on this beautiful animal. I took time to note the sounds and smells of the forest, and even the feel of the cold wind blowing against my skin. I was sure from that moment on there would be a reason to remember that fateful encounter with this king of the autumn woods.

The antlers of a dominant buck may differ substantially in formation depending on a variety of factors, including age, available nutrition, genetics and subspecies. These bucks are rare specimens indeed with antlers scoring well over 200 Boone and Crockett points. It is estimated that only one buck in 100,000 attains this size of antler development.

Autumn is a season of change, color, shorter days and frosty mornings. It is a time for magic and majesty, when the great kings of the species, the truly magnificent dominant males, appear and disappear in the blink of an eye. It is this moment, a fleeting second in time, when memories are etched into the minds of all who pursue the mighty whitetail buck.

Autumn's beginning is signaled by the onset of hardened antlers, preparation for the rut and an increase in social contact between the various herd members. Though primarily a solitary animal for most of the year, in fall the whitetail buck is most visible.

RISING FROM THE ASHES

O f all God's creatures great and small, the white-tail deer is surely His finest work of art. Few wild animals are as revered. Few fascinate so many people as does the whitetail buck, especially the giants of the species that are addressed in this book. The monarch's popularity can be attributed to many factors. Few animals in the world surpass his beauty, grace, and majestic appearance. His extensive range—from Canada to South America—and his ability to co-exist with man has made him accessible to a vast segment of the population. At the same

Rarely venturing into the open, whitetail bucks often throw caution to the wind during the breeding season or rut as it is called. They may travel miles from their home range in search of receptive does, a behavior that has led to the demise of many a mighty whitetail buck.

time, his secretive, reclusive nature adds to his mystique as one of the most crafty and elusive big game animals in the world.

Every autumn, these magnificent animals thrill thousands of hunters, photographers, and nature lovers from all walks of life. The sighting of one of these majestic creatures leaves a lasting, indelible image in the mind of any person who is fortunate enough to observe them, if only for a fleeting moment. Even if you have seen a thousand bucks, you will never forget the sighting of your biggest buck.

Few other animals have successfully adapted to and benefited from man's encroachment into their environment. With the demise of many of the whitetail's natural predators, man has assumed the major role in the management of this species. Unlike the elk and mule deer populations, whitetail numbers have increased dramatically as a result of man's intrusion. Across North America, whitetail deer numbers on the whole have risen for decades. The individuals featured in this book, however, are rare indeed, representing a very tiny percentage of the herd in any given area. In fact, in areas of North America with poor habitat and age structure, these giants are non-existent.

The antlers of the whitetail buck have fascinated mankind for centuries. Native Americans used these appendages as ceremonial implements, and as tools that were essential to their day-to-day existence and survival. Modern man has found assorted uses for antlers as well, turning them into jewelry, knife handles, and furniture ornamentation. In some countries, deer antler is believed to have medicinal and aphrodisiac properties. However, those for whom the whitetail holds the greatest attraction are the hunters, photographers, and nature lovers who journey to the outdoors by the millions each year, seeking this magnificent animal.

Whitetail deer have been proclaimed America's ultimate wildlife success story. Their present-day numbers, approximately eighteen to twenty million animals, are a tribute to one of the finest conservation efforts ever undertaken in North America. However, the future did not always look so bright. Some researchers estimate that as many as thirty-two million whitetails roamed North America around 1500 A.D., when explorers from Europe first came to the New World. However, the increased pressure and demands from New World settlers took an immediate toll. During the next three hundred years, the overall white-tail population declined by over fifty percent to approximately fifteen million animals.

Many factors contributed to this decrease, but the fur and hide trade, fueled by the demand for quality leather in Europe, must be considered a primary influence. Historical records document the tremendous numbers of deer hides exported from the colonies during the 1700s and 1800s. As an example, a port in Charleston, South Carolina, exported an average of more than 150,000 hides per year between 1739 and 1765. There were scores of similar export sites located on the Eastern seaboard and on up into Canada.

In addition, the movement of settlers west and the need for wild game for subsistence drastically cut into the existing population. Native Americans had subsisted on the whitetail deer for centuries, and had developed hunting and land use practices beneficial to the whitetail. Their ability to effectively harvest deer in large numbers to meet their daily needs is well documented. Although some historians and artists have painted a picture of the American Indian stalking a single whitetail buck in the North Woods with the bow and arrow as his only weapon, this was not always the case. Native American hunters were adept at this practice, but it was not time-efficient, yielding modest results for the amount of time and energy expended. These skilled hunters were much more proficient at herding or directing large numbers of deer into an

ambush site or enclosure, so large-scale harvesting could be done with minimal time and effort. Harvest techniques included the use of fire, dogs, large bodies of water, enclosures, snares, traps, and even poison to assure the reaping of large quantities of meat and hides. In many cases, hunting was a communal effort rather than an individual undertaking.

For centuries, the life of the American Indian was more dependent on the whitetail deer than on any other animal, including the bison. Though some argue that the bison was the most important big game species, its influence was limited to the sparsely populated Great Plains. By contrast, whitetail deer were spread throughout most of the North American continent. It must also be noted that the bison became a major source of subsistence only after American Indians mastered the use of the horse, which was reintroduced into North America by the Spanish in the late sixteenth century. Until that time, the preferred source of meat for the majority of tribes was the whitetail deer.

Native Americans pressed every ounce of the whitetail into service as clothing, blankets, tools, weapons, arrowheads, eating utensils, medicine, agricultural implements, glue, jewelry, ceremonial ornaments, and other instruments. The hide and antlers were the two parts most frequently used, but no part of the animal was wasted—including the entrails. Had this con-

servation-minded philosophy remained unchanged, whitetail numbers would probably have remained constant and healthy. However, as history has taught us, this was not the case.

As settlers and pioneers pushed west, the trade in fur and hides, the need for food, and modifications in land use affected whitetail populations. Native American attitudes toward the game changed as well. Various theories for this change in philosophy exist, but they do not completely explain why the whitetail suddenly became a commodity to be traded and exploited by not only the European settler but the American Indian as well. In most circles today, the American Indian is viewed historically as a conservationist—a view that is probably accurate as it pertains to the pre-settlement era. Inexplicably, a transition in their philosophy occurred that led to willing participation in the wholesale slaughter of the whitetail for economic reasons. European businessmen undoubtedly exploited the efficiency of the American Indian as a hunter, and the impact on whitetail herds was significant. Though the overall population was drastically reduced, it was by no means destroyed during this period. The estimated fifteen million animals present around 1850 still represented a sizeable population by anyone's standards.

The near-fatal blow was dealt in the relatively short time span of fifty years, between 1850 and 1900. During this time,

Rising from the Ashes

Over 30 million whitetails roamed North America when European settlers first arrived in the New World around 1500 A.D. By 1900, only about 350,000 animals remained. Today, the whitetail deer is deemed America's greatest conservation success story with over 20 million animals now living in North America.

which was characterized by the westward expansion of the railroad, the whitetail was hunted for commercial purposes. Venison was sold across the counter in much the same way beef is sold today. Even though beef became more available in the marketplace, venison remained the preferred meat of the American settler. Its popularity, coupled with a new wave of European interest in buckskin and the improvements in firearms during this period, led to the total elimination of the whitetail from most of its native habitat. By the time the damage

was halted near the turn of the century, it is estimated that there were approximately 350,000 whitetail deer remaining in all of North America. To place this in perspective, there are currently more than four million deer in the state of Texas alone.

Although game laws and hunting restrictions were placed on the books of virtually every state as early as 1646, the laws were rarely enforced. However, this changed when the Lacey Act was passed in 1900. This federal law prohibited the interstate transportation of illegally taken game,

When alarmed, it is easy to see how the whitetail earned its name. In many instances, this is the only view a great buck may offer his pursuer.

effectively curtailing the commercial hunting of all game animals. The Lacey Act was instrumental in reversing the plight of the whitetail deer.

In the early part of this century, efforts to conserve the whitetail were initiated, but they moved slowly due to many factors, including a lack of manpower and funds to finance large-scale restocking efforts. In fact, the first half of this century was in reality the darkest hour for this great animal. By 1937, very little progress had been made in restoring the great herds that had

once roamed the countryside. However, with the passage of the Pittman-Robertson Act that same year, funds were made available for wildlife management initiatives that included massive restocking programs and more effective management practices. This, combined with stricter hunting regulations, effective hunting practices, and enforcement of state game laws, fueled the tremendous revival of whitetail numbers nationwide.

Today, as we enter the twenty-first century, whitetail numbers approach those

31

Rising from the Ashes

seen over three hundred years ago. Even more encouraging is the fact that they are now expanding their range into areas where they have not been seen in the last century. In the mountainous states of the West, traditionally home for the elk and mule deer, the whitetail is now a common sight along many river valleys and waterways. In some areas, such as the Yellowstone River Valley, all three species co-exist on the same range during many months of the year.

Of all the wild animal species present in North America, the whitetail deer has become the most popular. Whitetails evoke strong emotions among both hunters and non-hunters, and both groups often claim this animal as their own symbol of all that is wild in our great land. Their universal appeal creates considerable controversy at times as to how their burgeoning numbers should be controlled. Effective management of the species is greatly hampered by our society's inability to separate the human values we have ascribed to the whitetail from the actual facts derived from scientific study about the animal's biological needs and behavior.

Many wildlife biologists and game managers believe that proper education of the general public, including hunters and anti-hunters, is essential to the continued success and health of the whitetail deer population nationwide. Misconceptions about the deer's biological needs, behavior, and status on the part of both extremes could have tremendous effect on shaping the views of the non-hunting public in general. It is feared that political decisions made in the future, influenced primarily by the non-hunting public, will dictate many of the management practices that control the fate of this magnificent animal. Continued success in the management of the species is dependent on continued research and education.

It can be argued that few animals symbolize as many things to as many people as the big dominant males of this species. Ask a hundred people for one word to describe the whitetail buck and you will get a hundred different answers. *Majestic, beautiful, noble, magnificent, stately, distinguished, impressive,* and *heart-stopping* are but a few of the common superlatives. However, no one word captures all that needs to be said about this fascinating creature. We have learned that he is an animal with a very complex personality that changes dramatically with the seasons. The docile, timid, and reclusive demeanor typical of the buck in spring and summer is in stark contrast to the foreboding, aggressive, dominant side that materializes during fall and winter. To say the least, he is a four-legged Jekyll and Hyde.

It has only been in the last three decades that substantial progress has been made in understanding the whitetail's biology, sociology, and behavior. We have learned that the social structure of the

whitetail deer is far more developed than once believed. Within healthy herds, the existence of dominant members from both sexes that govern the actions of subordinate herd members is somewhat similar to social structures in many of the canine species, such as the wolf and coyote. The dominant male, or alpha buck, attains his status through tactics that the general public does not necessarily associate with deer. He rises to his lofty position through the use of brute force and intimidation. Not only is he physically and psychologically superior to all other males within his territory, he is the most skilled male within the herd in both fighting and courtship. He is on the one hand a gladiator and on the other Don Juan.

Many studies have shown convincing evidence that whitetail does favor these large-antlered, mature dominant bucks over their younger and smaller counterparts, and may even select them as mates. It is believed that does are able to discern which bucks are dominant through a complex chemical communication process, and can determine the bucks' overall health and well-being prior to breeding. This mate selection process is extremely important to the health of our deer herds, and is nature's way of ensuring that only the healthiest, most genetically superior animals participate in the breeding process.

Although in many instances the mature alpha buck is an individualistic creature who keeps to himself most of the year, whitetails in general possess a highly developed social structure. Behaviors have evolved that permit them to communicate and interact with other bucks and does without actually having direct visual contact. Through behaviors known as signposting, dominant alpha bucks can advertise their presence to does in the herd and confirm their position as the breeding male within the territory.

Many other social behaviors have evolved within the whitetail that facilitate an orderly and efficient means of survival for the species. These behaviors allow the whitetail to exploit resources for optimal survival while minimizing herd stress and the destructive consequences of competition. It is a fascinating arrangement that biologists and researchers have only recently begun to unravel.

◀ Soon after shedding velvet, dominant bucks may make social visits to different doe family groups even before the rut is under way. The dominant males will patrol their territory on a regular basis, leaving a complex system of signposts and scents, which advertise his presence to all other members of the herd.

The role of the natural predator in most instances has been significantly diminished in most parts of the country, with man assuming the primary role of "herd manager." However, in some regions predators such as the wolf, mountain lion and coyote still play a significant role in the management of our whitetail herds. The removal of sick or weakened animals through natural predation can have an overall positive effect on the long-term health of the herd.

▲ This beautiful south Texas typical sports what is known as a drop tine. This odd antler characteristic has puzzled researchers for years.

◄ Though not considered a predator, the javalina co-exists with the white-tail in many parts of the southwest. At worst, he may be considered little more than a nuisance.

THE AUTUMN KING

Autumn is a season of fascination for whitetail enthusiasts. For many, it is more than just a season, it is an experience. It is a time for adventure and exploration, and a time to dream. It is a season of change, color, shorter days, and frosty mornings. It is also the period of time when the whitetail buck is most visible.

Autumn's beginning is signaled by the onset of hardened antlers, preparation for the rut, and an increase in social contact between the herd members. It is a time for magic and majesty, when the great kings of the species appear and

disappear in the blink of an eye. It is during this moment, a fleeting second for most of us, that memories are etched into the minds of all who pursue the mighty whitetail buck.

Many of these great whitetail monarchs have been documented over the past one hundred years with antlers so enormous that they defy imagination. Bucks such as the Brean, the Jordan, The Hole-in-the-Horn, and the Missouri Monarch are legendary animals who attract the attention and admiration of whitetail enthusiasts from around the world. Over the past century, millions of bucks have come and gone, but only a handful of animals have earned the kingly status attained by these legends of the autumn woods.

Regrettably, no one was ever fortunate enough to capture any of these legendary bucks on film prior to their demise. However, technological advances in film and photographic equipment over the past thirty years have filled this void with magnificent images of many great whitetail bucks similar to those featured in this work. These images have fueled the interest of the general public from coast to coast.

In 1996, the whitetail world was awakened by yet another giant buck who will certainly take his place among the greatest

◀ As soon as the process of velvet shedding is complete, all bucks will engage in pushing and shoving matches known as sparring.

The Autumn King

▲ The elusive, cunning nature of a big whitetail buck allows him to appear and disappear like a ghost in the night.
▶ The 1997 version of "30.30," perhaps the greatest whitetail buck ever photographed on the North American continent. Over 44 inches wide, no buck recorded in the current *Records of North American Whitetail Deer* comes close to his remarkable dimensions.

whitetails that ever lived. A hunter did not kill this buck. Nor were his antlers discovered in the wild after an untimely death due to predation or natural causes. This buck was alive, and his majesty will forever be recorded on film for all whitetail enthusiasts to enjoy. Photographs of this mighty buck, known as 30.30, adorn this book in several chapters. Nicknamed "The Autumn King," he became the inspiration for this project.

Decades ago, whitetail bucks achieved such popularity as trophies that a scoring system was developed by the Boone and Crockett Club to measure and record the remarkable growth of their antlers. The Boone and Crockett Club itself was established in 1887 by Teddy Roosevelt as an organization committed to the conservation of wildlife in North America. Its scoring system, developed many years later, has long been accepted as the standard for measuring the antlers of whitetail bucks, as well as for many other species around the world. Other recordkeeping organizations, such as Pope and Young for bowhunters, use the procedures and rules developed by

the Boone and Crockett Club. Buckmaster's Full Credit System follows basically the same procedures but differ on some of the finer points.

In order to develop an appreciation of the great bucks featured in this book, it is important to understand a few simple concepts about the Boone and Crockett scoring system. Simplified, the score is the sum of the inches of antler that a buck grows in one year. Measurements are made of the length of the points or tines, the length of the main beams, the circumference or mass at four specific spots on each beam, and the spread or width between the main beams. These measurements are added together and, after following some tricky guidelines and rules, a Boone and Crockett score is obtained.

The most common whitetail antler configuration is referred to as a "typical" formation and is found on the overwhelming majority of bucks. The graceful lines, the agile sweep of the beams, and the long, arching tines create an overall appearance unequaled by any other horned or antlered species in the world. Typical antlers are characterized by long, curving main beams that arise from "pedicles" on the skull plate and grow up, out, and forward. The points or tines will grow in a roughly ninety-degree angle upward from the beams, and will have a minimal number of abnormal points, or "kickers" as they are sometimes called. With this configuration, left to right antler symmetry is normal—a

consideration when computing the overall Boone and Crockett score. Deductions are taken for extra points that may extend from any place on the main typical frame, unbalancing the symmetry.

The less common formations are referred to as non-typical antlers. These formations involve large numbers of extra points as well as other oddities that can make them distinctly different than the typical-framed animals. Viewing these two antler forms side by side is somewhat like beholding Beauty and the Beast. The typical, with his elegant, graceful turns, long, sweeping beams, and symmetry, stands in stark contrast to the irregular, twisting, gnarly form presented by the non-typical. As the old saying goes, one has class, the other character.

There are as many non-typical formations as there are imaginations to dream them up. They normally have what is referred to as typical main frame development; however, it is accentuated with numerous other point formations. These include but are not limited to pearls, thorns, kickers, stickers, split points, cactus points, double main beams, drop tines, bifurcation, palmation, and formations that have yet to receive names. These extra inches are added into the final Boone and Crockett score rather than deducted from it as would be the case with typical formations. Only a very small percentage of bucks develop non-typical antlers. They are

The typical antler formation is characterized by elegant graceful turns, long sweeping beams and symmetrical tines.

The non-typical stands in stark contrast to the typical, often possessing gnarly, twisting, protruding antler formations that add "character" to his rack.

more common in older bucks, leading some experts to believe that allowing more bucks to attain maturity within a given herd would increase the occurrence of non-typical formation.

The magic score, or total inches, that must be accumulated by a buck's antlers to qualify for entry in the prestigious Boone and Crockett Record Book are 170 total symmetrical inches for the typical and 195 total inches for the non-typical. It is estimated that fewer than one out of every one hundred thousand bucks attains this level

of antler development. Many people consider bucks that reach this size nothing more than a freak of nature. However, to the whitetail enthusiast they are one of Mother Nature's rarest prizes.

Until recently, only two bucks had ever officially exceeded the 300-point barrier. That is just two bucks out of the millions that have existed in the past century. They lived out their lives in total secrecy, and both were discovered dead. The world-record non-typical, known as the "Missouri Monarch," was found dead by the side of a

road a short distance outside of St. Louis, Missouri, in 1981. It is believed that this buck, which amassed more than 333 total Boone and Crockett points, died of natural causes rather than injury from a passing vehicle. When officially scored, the buck shattered the existing world record by almost 50 points. Most outdoorsmen were astounded that such an animal could exist in relatively close proximity to such a large city. Shortly afterward, in 1983, the antlers of a second buck were discovered; the buck had apparently been killed by a train in 1940. Unknown to the world, the antlers had hung for more than 40 years in an Ohio sportsman's club. Due to a small hole penetrating a large drop tine, the deer was named the Hole-in-the-Horn buck. It was officially scored at over 328 inches.

What a wonderful sight it would have been to see these two magnificent animals sporting their enormous antlers in all their glory. One picture here would certainly have been worth more than a thousand words. However, bucks like these are one of the rarest occurrences in nature, and photographing them is near impossible even under the best of circumstances. It is this scenario that makes the discovery of 30.30 and the recording of the great buck on film a once in a lifetime experience for all who take pleasure in the sight of these magnificent animals.

While not the largest ever documented, 30.30's antlers may have been the most remarkable ever grown by a whitetail buck. As a representative of the non-typical category, he had two distinctions never seen in a whitetail close to his size—near-perfect symmetry and a near world-record typical main frame. The left antler contained ninety-three inches of typical growth, while the right side accumulated ninety-one and six-eighths inches, a difference of only one and two-eighths inches. (All Boone and Crockett scoring is recorded in one-eighth-inch increments.) It is his extraordinary size and exceptional balance that make him one of the most beautiful creatures ever recorded on film.

His overall dimensions were staggering: tine length up to sixteen inches, beams in excess of thirty-one inches, outside spread over thirty-nine inches, and an inside spread of thirty inches. Can there be any question as to how the buck earned his name? His final non-typical Boone and Crockett score of 301⅝ would have ranked him number three in the current record book, but antlers shed by living bucks are not eligible for inclusion. Even more impressive was the score of his eight-point typical main frame. At 211⅝ inches, it was within one and one-half inches of the current world record. To put his overall size in perspective, he would have been an exceptional elk!

In 1997, 30.30 once again stunned whitetail enthusiasts worldwide by growing a set of antlers with dimensions that surpass

The 1987 sheds from "Mr. Big." All male deer shed their antlers annually in early spring. New growth is generated by the buck in an amazingly short period of time, making antler one of the fastest growing tissues known to man.

any recorded buck in history. Though the overall appearance of these antlers was drastically different than the 1996 formation, they were a sight to behold. The total outside spread of these antlers surpassed an unheard of forty-four inches in width. No whitetail has ever come close to this dimension. His inside spread of over thirty-seven inches was wider than any buck in the current Boone and Crockett record book. The main beam measurements also exceeded those of any buck measured and recorded in the record book prior to that date.

What does the future hold for the great whitetail monarchs like 30.30 that still inhabit North America? Given proper education of the general public, effective management practices that take into account the overall health of our deer herds nationwide, and a reassessment of the human values we have assigned to this magnificent animal, the future is very bright indeed. In the twenty-first century, we may see whitetail herds rivaling those that existed when the first settlers stepped ashore in the New World over five hundred years ago.

◄ Mature, dominant bucks differ sharply from younger males in many aspects of their behavior including courtship. Younger males engage in what is commonly referred to as chase behavior while dominant bucks have a much easier time winning the attention of receptive does. Some studies have shown that receptive does seek out and favor these large dominant males as mates.

THE RISE TO DOMINANCE

From his meager beginnings, the life of a whitetail buck is a complicated and precarious one at best. His survival dictates that he must learn a great deal in a relatively short period of time. His environment will, to a large degree, define many of the behaviors he needs to acquire if he is to survive to maturity. Life in the "brush country" of deep south Texas is nothing like that endured by the bucks living in the far northern reaches of Canada or deep in the flooded swamps of Florida. For example, whitetails in the far northern latitudes learn to migrate

with the change in seasons, a behavior that is not necessary in warmer southern latitudes.

Initially, buck and doe fawns live a similar existence, both dependent on their mothers for all of life's necessities. Both sexes begin to learn about social order, dominance, and communication from their mothers and other older females within the matriarchal family group. This congregation is led by a dominant matriarch—a position determined by age, seniority, aggression, and the ability to produce and defend healthy offspring.

Typically, after a gestation period of approximately 200 days, twin fawns are born in the spring of each year. The timing of the fawning period varies from north to south; in the northern latitudes, the window of opportunity for producing fawns that will survive to maturity is very narrow. Young born outside of this time frame are at greater risk as winter approaches and may not survive the harsh cold and deep snows typical of this region. On the other extreme, fawns born in the south have a much wider time span for development. They may be born in late summer and still survive the mild winters common to these latitudes. Mortality in fawns can be substantial in any given year, based upon the combined effects of weather, the environment, predation, and other natural causes.

During the first two weeks of their lives, these fawns are extremely inactive.

59

The Rise to Dominance

▲ Young fawns develop very rapidly and by the time they are two weeks old, they are capable of eluding most predators on their own.
◄ Newborn fawns are extremely inactive and spend the overwhelming majority of their time hidden in seclusion. This low level of activity increases the likelihood that they will not be discovered by a passing predator.

They spend the large majority of their time in seclusion, hidden away by their mothers for their own protection from predators. The first two weeks are the most critical and vulnerable for the newborn fawns, and low levels of activity make it less likely that a fawn will draw the attention of a passing predator. Growth rates during this period of inactivity can be dramatic, with healthy fawns gaining up to ½ pound per day. By the time the fawn is fourteen days old, it is capable of eluding most predators on its own.

Most studies have shown that there is little statistical difference in weight between the sexes at birth. However, within the first month, the young buck fawn begins to grow more quickly than his female counterpart. By four months of age, the young fawns have been weaned from their mother's milk and are capable of foraging on their own. As their activity level increases so does their visibility, making the less healthy fawns more susceptible to predation by coyotes, bobcats, wolves, and even free-ranging domestic dogs.

Under normal circumstances, the first year of the buck's existence is spent within the maternal family group. The fawn's first

The Rise to Dominance

exposure to dominance and aggression is most likely learned within this social structure and may be exhibited as a part of play behavior. If born to a dominant matriarch, fawns quickly learn that she can be a fierce defender of their newfound position within the herd. Although she lacks antlers, a doe can more than make up for this deficiency with her feet. A kick from a mature doe, delivered to the head of an intruding underling, creates a very painful learning experience.

In addition to instinct and biology, learning begins to shape and mold the personality of the young males. They tend to be more active and curious than their female counterparts. Although some buck fawns are capable of producing very small antlers and breeding in their first season, this phenomenon is rare and reflects poor herd dynamics. As long as healthy, mature, dominant bucks exist in the herd, they will perform the majority of the breeding.

Aggression in bucks is a condition that is paramount to the survival of the species. Since the buck fawn, like his mother, lacks antlers, he performs his initial aggressive actions with his feet and legs, and through learned body language. Some sparring or head butting may occur between young males that grow small antlers as fawns. As a buck fawn progresses to a yearling, he will become a more proficient fighter and can deliver a painful blow to a rival that may result in severe injury.

Buck fawns learn different forms of body language than the does, and these are displayed in an attempt to assert dominance over other members of the social group. They include posturing and body language such as the stare, the hard look, the ear drop, and the head high and head low positions, all of which are used to intimidate a rival or younger, smaller member of the social group. As the buck matures and rises in status within the herd, he will begin to perfect his body language to such an extent that it often becomes the only tool he needs to maintain his position of dominance.

Yearling bucks undergo dramatic changes during their second autumn. These changes must be quite confusing for the young male, as his entire life is disrupted by several factors, including the appearance of newborn fawns at mother's side and, later in the fall, the onset of the rut. Alterations in the buck's body chemistry are triggered by the change in the amount of daylight, or the photoperiod. As the days begin to shorten, the lower light levels stimulate the production of testosterone in all bucks. The effect on the young buck is significant, including the formation of hardened antlers, the maturation of sex organs, and an increase in aggression toward other males. The small antlers he possesses in his first year are not impressive, and he will appear quite inept in his attempts to spar or impress the does or older bucks. He is both

The matriarchal family group is led by a dominant doe, a position determined by seniority, age, aggression and the ability to produce and defend healthy offspring.

physiologically and psychologically inept, and will quickly fall prey to the intimidation tactics forthcoming from the more mature bucks in the herd.

At this point in his physical development, the overall appearance of an immature yearling is starkly different than that of the older mature males. The differences are not unlike those seen in humans as they physiologically mature. Like many young teenagers, yearlings have very lean, thin bodies with little accumulation of body mass or fat. Their faces are thin and narrow. The back, between the withers and the

hips, and the belly area are very flat and straight. Their legs are rather thin as well.

As the young buck begins to mature, increased levels of testosterone foster noticeable changes in the muscle mass and bone structure. These changes are most evident in his face and his overall body mass. The face of an older mature buck is broad and heavy compared to his younger cohorts. Body mass increases significantly, with a noticeable sag in the belly region. The back will develop a bit of an arc, the effect of gravity on the extra body mass. Older bucks may even develop gray hairs

The Rise to Dominance

Young males normally remain with the maternal social group for their first year at which time they will normally leave or be forced out on their own, a process known as dispersal.

on the face around the muzzle, on the forehead, or around the eyes.

During early autumn, most yearling bucks either leave or are forced from the maternal social group. It was once believed that yearlings were generally driven from their birth areas by older mature bucks, but does within the social group—and more specifically the yearlings' mothers—play a highly significant role in this process.

The process is known as dispersal, and it requires that the young male establish relationships with bucks outside of the territory where he was born and raised. Young bucks enter a new social classification, taking on a role commonly referred to as that of a "subordinate floater." A young male may travel great distances before finding a home within a new fraternal social group. He may in fact visit many fraternal bands before finally gaining acceptance in one group.

The older bucks encountered by the yearling in this new fraternal social group are more sexually mature, and thus produce much higher levels of testosterone. As a result, they are far more aggressive and

Once accepted into a bachelor group, the younger males will socialize and learn valuable skills such as sparring and body language. As the buck matures, these skills become valuable aids in establishing the dominant-subordinate relationships that must exist in the fraternal social group.

intimidating than any doe the young male may have encountered in the maternal group. Aggression and intimidation are the enforcers of the social order and the dominant-subordinate relationship that must exist within the herd. Herein lies the key to the survival and health of the herd. The aggressive, more physically developed and skilled animals will become the predominant breeders and thus will pass on their genes to future generations. The weaker, inept, and unskilled bucks become subordinate and normally will not engage in the breeding of does. The process of natural selection, as well as the reality of the survival of the fittest, reign supreme in the whitetail community.

With acceptance in a fraternal social group, the young buck begins to learn many new facets of existence and survival. In his first couple of years within the group, he will most likely be relegated to a lower subordinate position but will socialize with more mature males. The core groups are small, normally containing no more than three to six members.

The Rise to Dominance

Dominance and aggression are learned behaviors necessary to the survival of the whitetail deer. These behaviors are essential in establishing a buck's position in the social order, an important process that determines who participates in the annual rut.

It is virtually impossible for a buck to enter the dominance hierarchy of a healthy herd until he is capable of competing both physically and psychologically with the older mature bucks. Depending on the age structure within the herd, this should occur when he is around four and one-half years old or older. By this age, bucks are more physically adept and sexually mature. Production of testosterone, the hormone that stimulates aggression in the male deer, increases with sexual maturity. Body growth in the form of mass becomes signif-

icant during the third and fourth seasons. The buck begins to gain confidence in his ability to spar and learns many of the intricacies of signposting behavior essential to future breeding success.

If circumstances are optimal, by age four the buck has reached a point in his physical development at which he is capable of competing with other mature bucks for the position of dominance within the social group. He will begin to challenge the dominant males and will acquire many new physical and psychological skills that will

enable him to rise within the social ranks. The acquisition of signposting skills, as well as other rut-related behaviors, will improve the buck's ability to communicate his higher position to other bucks and does alike. Through success in sparring and the use of learned body language, he will hopefully establish himself as a mature breeding male and begin the process of passing his superior genes on to the next generation.

Psychologically, the older buck is now capable of intimidating younger, immature bucks and will actively participate in suppressing their will to breed and their efforts to compete for higher social standing. His learned body language becomes instrumental in maintaining his higher rank. A mere look or stare from the dominant buck may be all that is necessary to discourage conflict or aggressive advances by younger bucks wanting to challenge his position.

The buck's physical skills have also matured, and he will be much more competitive in the sparring sessions that occur in early fall after velvet shedding. If successful in this arena, the buck will have completed his rise to dominance. Repeated challenges to his supremacy are inevitable; however, by the time the breeding season arrives, the dominant-subordinate roles of all bucks are established, and the rut begins as it has for thousands of years. The alpha buck assumes his role as a "dominant floater" and master of his domain.

The Rise to Dominance

◀ The spots in a fawn's coat are believed to serve as an aid in camouflage.
▲ Albino deer, such as this south Texas specimen (top) are extremely rare.
▲ By late August, the fawn will begin to shed its pelage of spots, replacing it with a much thicker winter coat that is essential to survival in the far northern latitudes.

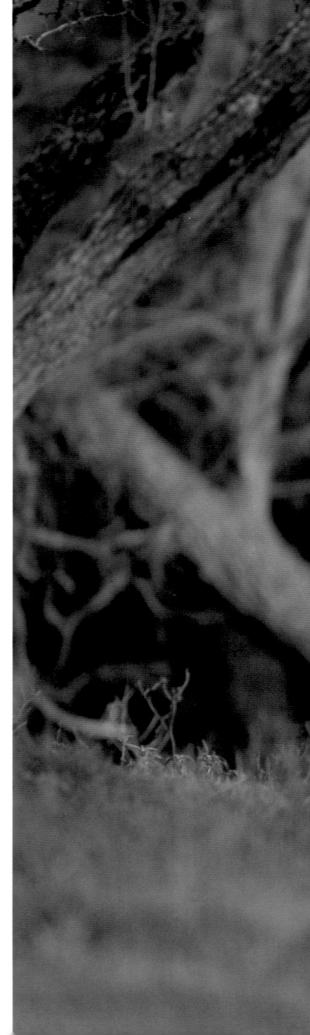

THE ALPHA BUCK

The alpha buck is the most dominant, aggressive male within his territory, and is typically the largest-bodied and most skilled in sparring and fighting. He most likely has the largest antlers and maintains a physical as well as psychological edge over every buck within his domain. This herd social status is normally earned by bucks five and one half years old or older, but it may be attained at an earlier age in herds from which most mature bucks have been removed due to hunting, predation, or other causes. Alpha bucks are also characterized by their highly skilled body language, ritualized courtship behavior, and intricate signposting skills.

Nature has devised an elaborate scheme that allows the whitetail deer to perpetuate the species based upon genetic superiority. Aggression and dominance are major ingredients in this plan. Once a mature male attains or earns the alpha buck status, he secures the primary role of breeding within his territory, though other high-ranking subordinate bucks will do some of the breeding while the alpha buck is busy tending a receptive doe. A pecking order is determined by each buck's social standing, so theoretically only bucks in the higher ranks will participate in the breeding process when healthy herd dynamics are in place.

This social order is established by a number of factors, including a buck's age, physical size, sparring skill, psychological and sexual maturity, and general overall health. Some dominant bucks that survived from the previous year will be displaced due to old age and an inability to stand their ground against other bucks that have entered their prime. Hunting and natural predation may remove many healthy mature bucks from the herd on an annual basis.

Many older dominant males become quite reclusive during this period of their life cycle and may spend the majority of their time removed from the larger fraternal social groups. All deer spend the majority of their time within a two- to three-square-mile area referred to as their home range. The home range is the living area of a deer under normal circumstances. It offers all of the essentials of life, including food, water, and cover. Larger home ranges are found in areas with lower population densities, such as the open range and northern latitudes. Smaller ranges are normally found under the opposite conditions but may also be influenced by the personality of an individual animal. Does normally have much smaller home ranges than bucks.

Soon after velvet shedding in early autumn, the alpha males must emerge from isolation in order to reaffirm or establish their position of dominance within the ranks. They begin to journey outside their home range and will drastically expand their travels during the rut. Social contact is of immense importance during early autumn, and all bucks become more visible as a result. Bucks may occasionally interact with doe groups in early autumn, especially around feeding areas that attract several different buck and doe family groups. Dominant bucks may even make short "social visits" to doe family groups prior to the onset of the rut.

Sparring bouts begin soon after bucks enter the hardened antler stage. Sparring differs from antler fighting in its intent, level of aggression, and eventual outcome. True antler fighting is generally a result of

conflicts over territory or breeding rights and occurs between equally matched dominant males during the breeding season.

The intensity of sparring increases as the primary rut approaches. Initially, bucks merely touch antlers and gently push—exercises directed at determining the size and shape of their antlers and how best to confront a challenger. The gentle pushing is eventually transformed into more physical bouts that can become quite serious. These confrontations always end with a winner and a loser. The winner gains a notch in the

dominance hierarchy; the loser becomes a subordinate and drops a position in the breeding order.

Depending on population densities, various problems confront the whitetail buck in his diverse needs to communicate with other deer in his territory. Once a buck establishes his rank of dominance within the fraternal social group, he must undertake the complicated task of advertising his position within the herd. He is required to communicate his position and his presence to all other deer within his territory. In the

A younger buck, probably two years old, challenges a much older buck to a sparring match. The older, more dominant buck accepts the challenge and entertains the younger male in a match of pushing and shoving. Viewed more correctly as a social interaction, rarely do these matches result in injury to either animal.

The use of signposting behavior is the dominant buck's vehicle for communicating his presence to the remainder of the herd. Here a buck "marks" an overhead limb with his nasal glands and saliva, an essential step in the process of establishing a scrape.

north, where deer densities are lower, deer are distributed over a wider range and may have fewer opportunities to visually access each member of the herd. In the south, communicating who is who within a territory becomes a problem because of the higher population densities, especially as the breeding season or rut approaches.

Dominant bucks successfully communicate information to other herd members within their territory through processes known as signposting. Although some level of signposting occurs throughout the year,

it is far more prevalent and visible during the rut. Signposting behavior causes the dominant buck to leave two very different indicators throughout his territory. These indicators communicate his physical presence, his social position or rank within the herd, and his intent to enforce his position. Rubs, areas on small trees that have been debarked by the buck with his antlers, and scrapes, pawed depressions in the earth left at the base of trees that contain an overhead marking limb, are the calling cards of the dominant males.

The Alpha Buck

Serving as both a visual and olfactory signpost, rubs are another essential part of the buck's complex chemical communication system. The buck applies chemicals from his forehead gland to the rub that not only advertise his presence to available does, but also serve to physiologically inhibit rutting behavior in subordinate males.

The rub serves as both a visual and olfactory signpost. Depending on his personality, the alpha buck may establish hundreds of these rubs across his territory. Large numbers of rubs may be clumped together in certain areas due to abundant food, open cover, preferred trees, and the availability of does in the area. Some initial rubbing occurs as velvet is being shed, but it is the rubbing associated with the rut that the buck uses as a chemical communication system to advertise his presence. It is much akin to your pet dog's visit to the fire hydrant.

The buck deposits chemicals present in his forehead gland on these trees, and these chemicals serve a dual purpose. They aid in letting does know that he is king of his domain and available for breeding when the appropriate time arrives. It is also suspected that these chemical markers have the effect of physiologically inhibiting rut behavior in subordinate males, diminishing competition and conflict between bucks within the herd.

Established as the rut approaches, scrapes are an even more complex form of

Whitetail Monarchs

This monstrous buck returned hourly to this cedar, working his antlers and forehead over the aromatic growth until all that was left was a small stub sticking up from the ground.

communication. A scrape is produced when the buck paws the ground, usually near the base of a tree, and urinates in the fresh earth. Chemicals deposited in the scrape as the buck urinates over the tarsal glands on his rear hocks do more than advertise dominance; they also communicate his readiness to breed. Studies indicate that chemicals present in the urine of dominant bucks may also inform does of the bucks' physical condition and whether they are healthy breeders. Researchers feel that a form of mate selection takes place when a

doe visits the scrape and advertises her willingness to breed with a specific male by urinating and stepping in the scrape. The buck is then able to follow the doe, rendezvous, and successfully breed.

The scrape is never complete unless an overhead marking branch is present above the scrape. This small limb, usually about head high to the buck, is a complicated tool in itself. The buck deposits scent from his pre-orbital and nasal glands, in conjunction with saliva, on the overhead limb. This deposit reveals his identity, while scent and

The Alpha Buck

Though all bucks participate in signposting to some degree, the process becomes far more ritualized in older dominant bucks, often resulting in very impressive rubs such as the one pictured on the facing page.

chemicals left in the scrape advertise his dominance, physical condition, and readiness to breed. Bucks perform some scraping and overhead branch marking year-round, but for reasons other than breeding. All bucks participate in some level of signposting, but the behavior becomes more developed and ritualized among older dominant males.

Scrapes and rubs probably evolved in the species as a result of the deer's highly developed olfactory senses. Deer have two systems for analyzing scent—the nose and

the vomeronasal gland. If you've spent much time around whitetail bucks during the fall, you have no doubt witnessed a buck in what is referred to as a lip curl position. More correctly called a flehmen posture, it is the means by which a buck stimulates his reproductive system. The process does not result in a determination by the buck that a doe is ready to breed. The chemicals analyzed by the buck through the vomeronasal gland indicate to the buck that the doe may be approaching estrus, and that he may initiate his courtship ritual in an attempt to win the doe's approval.

A buck actually does use his nose and olfactory nervous system to determine whether a doe is ready to breed. Older dominant males approach a doe in a series of head-down, neck-outstretched trots. The maneuver is reminiscent of the sight of a bird dog hot on the scent of a quail. By smelling the doe's urogenital area or the tarsal gland, the buck is able to determine if the doe is in estrus and ready to breed. If signals from the vomeronasal gland indicate that she is approaching estrus but the olfactory system indicates she has not quite reached that magical point, the buck stays close by the doe's side until breeding can be completed, which usually happens within thirty-six hours.

It is this complex chemical communication system that establishes much of the order the herd needs to successfully regenerate itself from year to year. It allows

The complex chemical communication system that results from signposting behavior is essential to the order necessary for the herd to regenerate itself. As a result, herd stress is minimized and the dominant buck's genes are successfully passed to the next generation.

dominant bucks to exercise control over subordinate males, minimizing the need for physical confrontation during the actual breeding season. It contributes to the over-all well-being of the herd by giving bucks and does an effective means of communicating their readiness to breed without actual physical contact. As a result, the presence of the dominant alpha buck is registered, and the passing of his superior genes to the next generation is virtually guaranteed.

85

The Alpha Buck

A buck is able to determine if a doe is ready to breed by smelling her urogenital area or the tarsal gland. If the buck concludes that the doe is not quite in estrous, he will stay close by her side until breeding can be completed, usually within thirty-six hours.

A CROWN FOR THE KING

The one characteristic that defines the whitetail deer as perhaps the most regal and beautiful of all the deer species is the crown of antlers he carries so majestically during the fall and winter of each year. Within the past three decades, research studies have isolated many of the factors that influence antler development in whitetail deer. We know a lot about the physiology of how antlers grow, and about the factors that allow them to grow to exceptional size.

There are three primary factors that researchers feel

91

Researchers believe antler development is influenced by three primary factors; age, nutrition, and genetics. However, factors such as stress, environmental conditions and psychology may have a substantial impact on the process as well.

influence antler development—age, nutrition, and genetics. Deficiencies in any of these influences will result in less than optimal antler growth. Other contributing factors, such as psychology and environmental conditions, can have tremendous influence on the process as well. However, many of the factors influencing *why* a particular buck grows an extraordinary set of antlers are still a mystery that confounds even the best of the experts.

Some studies indicate that dominance, and therefore psychology, significantly influences the antler development process. Bucks that attain dominance within the social structure differ sharply from subordinate younger bucks in many facets of antler development, including size, casting, the initial onset of growth, and the timing of velvet shedding. Their use of the hardened appendages in signposting and other rut-related functions differs as well. Through body language known as posturing, large dominant bucks stand with their heads high in a demonstrative manner, showing off their large antlers to both bucks and

A Crown for the King

does within the herd. Scientists believe this behavior inhibits subordinate males while attracting interested females.

The change in the photoperiod, which controls so much of the whitetail's biology, regulates antler development as well. Although the process is not entirely understood, the ratio of light to darkness plays a key role.

As the amount of daylight increases in early spring, antler growth is stimulated by a complicated interaction of several glands responsible for the secretion of hormones within the body. It is the lowering of testosterone in the male that triggers antler casting and thus the eventual onset of antler development in early spring. As the days of late summer begin to shorten, hormonal growth is accelerated, triggering the final development of the antler into its mineralized or hardened state. As days begin to lengthen in late winter, an increase in available light again triggers the process of casting and eventual antler regeneration.

Researchers have successfully induced bucks to grow as many as three different sets of antlers in one year simply by manipulating the ratio of light to darkness. Controlling this single factor allowed researchers to accelerate the cycle of regeneration, mineralization, and casting of antlers. However, the overall effect on the animal was extremely stressful. The bucks' systems were depleted of large quantities of calcium and other valuable minerals. An even more interesting finding is that, if the ratio of light to darkness is maintained as an unchanging constant, a buck will grow no antlers at all!

Antler is the fastest-growing bone known to man and is very similar to bone cancer in its cellular appearance and growth process. During the growth stage, antler possesses many of the same chemicals found in bone cancer cells. Hardened antler is solid bone and contains no inner marrow. It is grown only by the deer family, Cervidae, and the hardened antlers are shed annually. Antlers grow from the tips rather than from the bases, and they contain a blood and nerve supply during the growth process. They are unlike horns, which are composed of a protein called keratin, are not shed except in pronghorns, and grow annually from the bases. They also differ from horns in that they branch out and form multiple tines.

Antlers grow from formations on the buck's forehead known as pedicles, which normally develop while the buck is a fawn. Research has shown that without a pedicle, a buck will simply not grow antlers. Studies have also documented a correlation between the size of the pedicles and eventual antler size. The larger the pedicle, the larger the antlers eventually produced. Likewise, studies have shown a correlation between a buck's body size, his age, and antler development.

A normal growth cycle begins with the

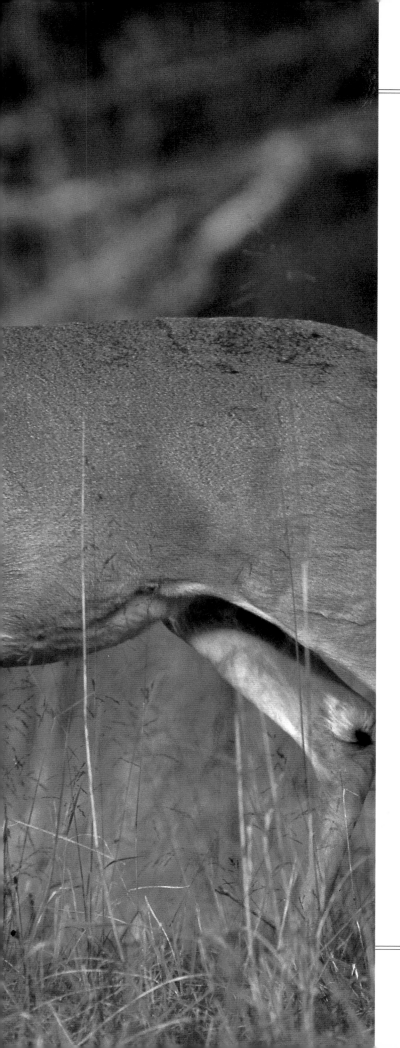

shedding of the previous year's antlers. The process of casting, as it is called, takes place earlier in the year in the northern latitudes and as late as March or April in the southern latitudes. The casting process leaves a wound that must heal before any new growth can occur. Dominant bucks tend to cast their antlers earlier than subordinate bucks, thus entering the new growth stage at an earlier date. However, this process can be sharply affected by a buck's overall health and by numerous other environmental factors that may stress the animal.

Documentation of 30.30's antler growth revealed that he routinely shed his antlers much earlier than other bucks, including the big two hundred-point bucks living in the same area. By early March, substantial antler formation had occurred, with over two hundred inches completed by mid-June. His three hundred-point antlers were completed by mid-July, although he shed his velvet at about the same time as all other bucks living in that part of the country.

A buck's casting wound heals within a short period of time, and velvet-covered bulbs begin protruding from the pedicle area. Initial growth is very slow; however, by late May or June in the northern latitudes (later in the South), growth accelerates remarkably. The antler grows approximately one-quarter inch per day, and even more in the large-antlered alpha bucks that can accumulate over two hundred inches of

97

A Crown for the King

Dominant bucks sometimes make short social visits with doe family groups prior to the onset of the rut in early autumn. The interactions may be more common around feeding areas that may attract several different buck and doe family groups into the same area.

total antler growth in less than four months.

During the entire developmental process, the antlers are covered by a soft, skin-like material known as antler velvet. The velvet has a rich blood supply and is well endowed with sensitive nerves. The velvet is comprised of thousands of tiny, hair-like follicles, and it actually feels like velvet to the touch. The velvet's skin produces an oily substance known as sebum, which gives the skin the very shiny appearance so often visible at the tips of tines. The

velvet and skin are pliable, accommodating the tremendous stretch and expansion that occurs in very large-antlered bucks.

The extensive nerve supply affects several aspects of the buck's antler development. The nerves give the buck some sense of the size and proportion of his antlers, thus minimizing his chances of bumping the antler and causing serious injury or deformity. In many instances, non-typical antlers are the result of injuries to the antler during the velvet stage or injuries to the pedicle itself.

During the velvet stage of antler development, most bucks can be found living in bachelor bands that may contain anywhere from three to sometimes more than eight bucks. The mood of the whitetail buck is far more docile during this time of the year, a condition that will change rapidly as velvet is shed and testosterone levels begin to rise.

Due to the sensitive nature of the antlers during this stage of development, bucks avoid antler contact completely. Disputes during this time period will be settled through body language or by standing on their hind legs flailing at each other with their front legs. The advanced body language skills associated with dominance are the preferred tactics in settling the confrontations that are so prevalent within bachelor groups during early antler development. The psychological edge enjoyed by the older males is apparent during any confrontation with a younger, less experienced subordinate.

The antler growth period extends into late July, or as late as mid-August in deep south Texas brush country. At this time, growth of the antlers subsides and the process of mineralization begins. The mineralization process, or hardening of the antler material, progresses from the pedicle toward the tips and from the outside of the antler inward, thus restricting the blood supply to the bone and finally shutting it off completely. With the restriction of

A Crown for the King

blood flow, the velvet's nutrient supply dwindles rapidly, and it quickly dies. The shedding or peeling of the velvet skin occurs as it shrinks and dries, thus leading to the death of the bone material itself. Mineralization and the death of the inner bone core is completed within a few weeks after the velvet is shed, thus completing the process of antler development.

For decades, velvet shedding has been shrouded in many misconceptions. It was once believed that the buck had to rub the velvet from his antlers in order to attain the clean appearance present in the hardened state. In fact, there seem to be individual differences among bucks regarding who needs to rub and who doesn't to achieve the final effect. Some bucks participate in vigorous rubbing activity to remove velvet, while others do no rubbing at all. In many instances, the velvet will simply die, split, and fall from the antlers with little if any assistance from the rubbing process. The early rubbing after velvet shedding does, however, seem to have an effect on antler coloration. Tree bark and sap darken the antler material, particularly in the area close to the bases. Bucks deprived of prime rubbing trees are often left with antlers that are extremely light in coloration.

Bucks may produce very small, hardened antlers as fawns. These are often referred to as "buttons." The males normally produce their first full set of antlers as yearlings. These antlers are very small and normally have only a few points. Yearling bucks with 10 points must be considered exceptional and uncommon animals. However, studies have shown that there is little correlation between the size of a buck's first set of antlers and those grown later. Some yearling bucks that grow only spike antlers eventually sport antlers of tremendous size, sometimes exceeding 200 Boone and Crockett points. These examples are far more common than one might assume. The occurrence of spike antlers is more often associated with poor overall nutrition or late fawn births rather than genetic inferiority, as was once commonly believed. The genetic occurrence of spike antlers in healthy mature whitetail bucks is extremely rare and may even be geographically isolated.

We know that it is basically impossible for a buck to grow a huge set of antlers in his first two to three years. Isolated cases of bucks that grew 170 inches of antler at the age of three years have occurred, but are extremely rare. Antlers of this size are more likely to be grown after a buck reaches maturity at age four, and are much more likely to develop when a buck enters his prime at five. If he maintains his health, he may continue to produce superb antlers into his eighth and ninth seasons, but rarely beyond. Tooth wear—and therefore poor nutritional intake—becomes a major contributor to this decline in later years. Other factors, such as reduced levels of testos-

terone production, injury, overall poor health, and stress also contribute to this decline.

Many researchers believe that overall antler development within a herd could be improved dramatically by allowing more bucks within a herd to develop to maturity. They believe that the genetic potential for exceptional antler development may be present in all herds, but may never materialize due to over-harvesting of immature bucks from these herds. Research studies aimed strictly at controlling this variable within a given herd certainly lend credence to this belief.

The Hagerman Refuge whitetail herd is an excellent example of just how significant a factor age is in antler development. Many bucks on the refuge reach maturity, due to several factors including bowhunting-only seasons in the area, low population densities, high agricultural usage, and exceptional cover. Although no official research on antler development has been conducted on the refuge, visual observation reveals that average mature whitetails consistently produce antlers in the one hundred and thirty to two hundred point range. Each fall, bucks scoring well above two hundred Boone and Crockett points are well documented in this area.

Conversely, one- and two-year-old bucks harvested during area bowhunts are not very large at all, as might be expected. Most are small-antlered, six- and eight-pointers that score under one hundred Boone and Crockett points. This would indicate that age may be the largest contributing factor in the antler development equation, meaning that if a buck is allowed to mature, he will grow significantly larger antlers. Genetics and nutrition certainly add to the equation; however, no matter how significant these two factors may be, a buck cannot be expected to grow exceptional antlers in his first two years.

Studies isolating nutrition and its effect on antler development have shown that nutrition is also a vital factor. The buck must have all the basic nutrients available, including protein, fats, carbohydrates, essential minerals such as calcium and phosphorus, and vitamins in order to maximize his potential antler development. Without proper nutrition, a buck will not maximize his antler development regardless of age, genetic predisposition, or rank within the social order. In areas where soil quality is inherently poor, it is virtually impossible for mature bucks to grow large antlers, due to a lack of nutritional and mineral intake. In these areas, even reducing the herd size and improving the amount of available food has little impact on antler quality. In areas where soil quality is exceptional, however, the occurrence of bucks with tremendous antler growth rises dramatically.

The potential for large antler development may also be determined to a great

A Crown for the King

Tremendous size and body mass are characteristic of most dominant bucks. They use their size as a physical as well as psychological advantage over subordinate bucks that may from time to time challenge their position of superiority within the herd.

extent by genetics. However, there are more questions than answers in assessing the influence of this variable. Studies show that many antler characteristics, including overall antler size, mass, shape, beam length, and the length and numbers of tines, are indeed heritable traits. Ranch managers, biologists, and researchers have manipulated genetics in breeding populations on private ranches with admirable results for several decades. However, the consistent production of Boone and Crockett-sized bucks in large numbers is still beyond the reach of most if not all of these programs.

The same problem exists in all animals that have been genetically manipulated to achieve the highest level of success, among them racehorses and cattle. Overall quality is generally improved, but why some animals achieve maximum development and others don't is one of nature's mysteries that we may never fully unravel. What *is* understood, though, is that the female in any given species is as important a contributor to genetic predisposition as the male, and may in fact be more important in influencing some of the antler characteristics of whitetail deer. Due to the fact that does do not normally produce antlers, it is difficult to visually assess this influence. For the time being, it can only be assessed by evaluating the eventual effect seen in her offspring as they mature.

One overlooked factor among many herd managers is the fact that the antler configuration displayed by a buck may not be an accurate representation of the genetic characteristics the buck actually carries and passes on to his offspring. What is shown outwardly in antler development—phenotype—and what is actually genetically present and transmitted to future generations—genotype—may be vastly different for a particular buck. The culling of a buck from a herd, if based on less-than-desirable antler size alone, may in fact eliminate quality genetics from that herd. Many other factors should be assessed before such a decision is made. As is the case with Thoroughbred racehorses, the fleetest horse may not turn out to be the greatest of sires. That role has often times fallen to a horse of lesser stature on the track. Likewise, a buck endowed with a less-than-desirable rack during a season may in fact be carrying superior genetics that will be passed on to his offspring.

Overcrowding can cause not only herd stress but stress on the individual bucks, and will inhibit or retard a buck's ability to produce antlers to his full potential. When herd size exceeds the carrying capacity of the land, prime forage is quickly eliminated and an entire herd can suffer dramatically from the effects of malnutrition and psychological stress. The Texas "Hill Country" is a prime example of this problem, producing bucks that rarely exceed one hundred pounds with very small antlers. In parts of the Hill Country that have been high-fenced to control population densities as well as age structure, however, individual deer grow to the normal body and antler size expected for the *texanus* subspecies.

Several studies have shown that late fawning dates may significantly influence antler development in many yearlings. The occurrence of spike-antlered bucks in a herd can often be attributed to this variable alone. In unhealthy herds that suffer from poor nutrition and high population densities, these late-born fawns may never reach full antler potential. However, in herds where sex and age structure is healthy and nutritious forage is abundant, these fawns usually catch up to their earlier-born cohorts in body size and antler development within a couple of years.

As indicated earlier, psychology is believed to play an important role in antler development as well. Dominant bucks, meaning bucks that are both psychologically and physiologically superior, are normally the first bucks within a herd to cast their antlers in late winter, thus entering into the antler regeneration process at an earlier date. They are also the first bucks to shed velvet and polish out their antlers. They use this to their advantage by psychologically stressing younger subordinate bucks within the herd. This psychological intimidation leads to physiological suppression of testosterone in the younger bucks, basically rendering them ineffective at breeding as long as dominant bucks are present in the herd.

Overall, this phenomenon has a positive effect on herd dynamics. Younger bucks are saved the physiological stress of breeding until their bodies are more mature. Competition and physical conflicts are minimized between many of the bucks, reducing the chance of death due to injuries and depletion of energy reserves. Does, on the other hand, breed with the physically superior alpha buck that has gained his lofty position by way of age, physical size, maturity, health, and the ability to demonstrate control over the fraternal society. He can thus spread his superior genes throughout his territory and contribute to the genetic health of the herd for generations to come.

Though the buck in the middle is substantially smaller in both body size and antler development, he was much older and enjoyed a psychological edge that allowed him to maintain his dominance over this particular bachelor group.

Whitetail Monarchs

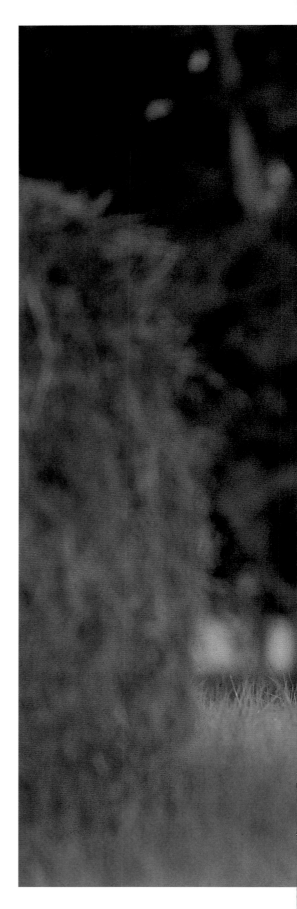

During the antler's growth stage, it is covered by a soft skin-like material known as velvet which has a very rich blood supply and is endowed with very sensitive nerves. The velvet covering is very pliable, allowing for tremendous stretch and expansion. In many instances, non-typical antlers are the result of injuries to the antler during the velvet stage.

The velvet is comprised of thousands of tiny hair-like follicles and actually does feel like velvet to the touch. The velvet's skin produces an oily substance known as sebum, which gives the skin a very shiny appearance visible at the tips of tines.

▶ Antler grows from formations on a buck's head known as pedicles. Correlation has been found between the size of antler pedicles and eventual size antlers a buck may produce.

THE LAND OF THE GIANTS

The whitetail deer, *odocoileus virginianus,* has basically remained unchanged since it appeared about four million years ago on the North American continent. As many as thirty-eight subspecies have been identified from Canada to South America, with seventeen distinct subspecies identified in the United States by 1940. However, because of the massive restocking programs conducted from the early 1900s into the 1980s, it is suspected that a great deal of hybridization of these subspecies has occurred, leaving the existence of these separate subspecies as pure strains in question.

117

Known for their tremendous body size and huge antlers, the *borealis* subspecies inhabit the midwest and northeastern regions of North America. This buck's live weight was estimated at over 400 pounds, large for even this subspecies.

For example, deer from Wisconsin (the Northern Woodland or *borealis* subspecies) were transplanted into Alabama, Arkansas, Florida, Georgia, Kentucky, Louisiana, Maryland, Mississippi, North Carolina, Tennessee, Virginia, and West Virginia. The genetic result of these transplants and thousands of others from different subspecies was undoubtedly the creation of many hybrid strains. Some states documented receiving transplanted deer from as many as nine other states, representing as many as five subspecies.

The larger subspecies, such as the *borealis* and *dacotensis*, are found in the far northern United States and Canada. The smaller species, the Key and Coues deer, are found in the southern parts of the whitetail's range, such as Florida and Arizona. This is consistent with a principle known to all wildlife managers as Bergmann's Rule. This rule states that warm-bodied species found in the colder northern climates will be larger in body size than their southern counterparts. According to the theory, the larger body size is a biological

adaptation aimed at more efficient retention of body heat during the severe winters common to this geographic area. The smaller-bodied deer found as one travels south are more efficient at dissipating heat during the severe summers common to the southern extremes. As with any rule, there are exceptions. However, Bergmann's Rule does seem to explain many of the physical differences seen in the whitetail deer from North to South.

Many studies have consistently shown that antler size is correlated to a large degree with body size. Bergmann's rule, then, can be used as an accurate indicator of where some monstrous whitetails may range in larger numbers. But it's not quite that simple. Other factors, such as soil conditions, population densities, available nutritious browse, and dense cover, must also be taken into consideration.

Related to Bergmann's Rule is another tendency noted by researchers in recent studies concerning east to west trends in antler development. It has been documented that, as one travels westward from the East Coast toward the center of the country, antler size on the average increases. The same trend is noticeable from the West Coast eastward. For instance, even though the South Texas whitetail subspecies, *texanus*, lives just as far south as the Florida Key deer and southwestern desert Coues deer, its antlers are substantially larger. The same trend is evident in moving from

Whitetail Monarchs

Virginia to Missouri and Kansas, from Pennsylvania to Illinois and Iowa, or from Maine to Minnesota.

One would then assume that if we start from the southeastern coastal region and move west and north through the central portion of the U.S. and Canada, we would locate the largest-antlered representatives of the whitetail species. The Boone and Crockett Record Book indicates that this assumption is valid. Of the top one hundred typical whitetails in the record book, all but six were produced by this geographic region. All six of those exceptions were produced in the state of Texas, again in the geographic center of the United States. Most of the largest bucks (and the largest overall number of record book entries) originated from the northern and central Corn Belt states of Wisconsin, Minnesota, Iowa, and Illinois, and northward into the Canadian provinces of Saskatchewan, Alberta, and Manitoba.

Researchers propose two explanations for this trend. The first may lie in the geography of the land itself. As one moves toward the West, the thick woodlands of the East are slowly transformed into the open agricultural lands of the Midwest and Great Plains. Large antlers may have evolved in response to this open country. They are more visible, and thus offer an advantage to dominant bucks in that they are more easily detected by other deer and serve as a greater deterrent to predators.

Does, attracted to the large-antlered bucks, would ensure that the bucks' genetics would become ingrained in the herd structure over time. The psychological advantage of the large antlers over subordinate bucks would be effective at a greater distance as well.

The large-antlered bucks would not fare as well in the densely covered forests found to the east. Overly large antlers in this type of geography inhibit general navigation and escape from predators. Even browsing for food could be a problem in the dense underbrush. The visual advantage of the larger antlers would also be obscured by the thick understory.

A second explanation for the existence of larger bucks in this geographic area may lie with the glaciers that covered the majority of this region during the Ice Age. Starting roughly two million years ago and ending as recently as ten thousand years ago, glaciers pushed south into North America from Canada. The mineral-rich sediment deposited in many areas by these glaciers was in time converted into the fertile soil now characteristic of this vast agricultural region. These nutrient- and mineral-rich soils are a major factor in the production of large deer antlers. Studies have shown that areas of the country devoid of quality soils consistently produce bucks with extremely poor antlers. Although attainment of maturity has some positive effect, introduction of quality genetics has

Tremendous antler mass such as this is rare in any whitetail subspecies; however, as a rule it is more common among bucks inhabiting the far northern latitudes.

little positive effect on the final outcome of antler development in these infertile areas.

Again, a quick study of the record book supports this supposition. When we overlay a map of the southernmost advances of the glaciers into North America, the area covered accounts for all but eight of the top one hundred typical bucks entered into the Boone and Crockett record book. Combining the effects of Bergmann's rule, the central continental effects, and the advances of the glaciers will account for all

but a handful of the top one hundred typical Boone and Crockett bucks.

One unique quality of the whitetail deer's antlers is that no two sets are exactly the same. They are in this respect similar to human fingerprints. Their characteristics can be so distinct that antlers can be used to identify individual animals. However, there is one characteristic common to the antlers of nearly all bucks that attain super antler growth. That characteristic is the extraordinary length of the main beams. According

The Land of the Giants

to the current *Records of North American Whitetail Deer* (1995 Edition), the thirteen entries with net scores over two hundred typical inches have beams that average an amazing twenty-eight and one-quarter inches in length. Bucks with typical formations amassing more than one hundred and ninety inches of symmetrical antler growth (the top 103 bucks recorded in this category) have an average beam length of over twenty-seven and one-half inches. While antler spread, the number and length of tines, and the amount of mass may vary tremendously among these animals, beam length remains remarkably constant in the larger specimens, comprising on average about thirty-two percent of their total Boone and Crockett score. Variation of this statistic appears to be very slight, as nearly seventy-three percent of all typical bucks fall within two percent of this figure. Of the top one thousand bucks listed in the typical category, only one animal had an average main beam length of less than twenty-two inches. Further analysis shows that as bucks add less than one inch of growth to both beams, average total Boone and Crockett scores increase by an average of ten inches.

It is possible that for decades, game managers have been selecting the wrong antler characteristics in managing deer herds for superior antler development. When examined closely, the record book data indicates tremendous variations in tine length and number, mass or circumference measurements, and inside spread of the main beams. This wide variation is lacking when we look at main beam development and the relationship of this factor to overall antler development. Extraordinary main beam length is clearly the defining antler characteristic for all typical Boone and Crockett whitetails. Bucks with ten or more points averaging over twenty-seven inches in main beam development stand an excellent chance of scoring over the 170 minimum inches necessary to make the record book.

In summary, it may be said that where corn is king, so is the whitetail buck. The larger-bodied bucks indigenous to the Corn Belt region consistently produce the largest antlers. However, other areas of the country with nutrient- and mineral-rich soils will also produce large-antlered bucks. This holds true whether we are looking in the Deep South or the far north.

Nature's plan for dealing with the aggressive dominant nature of whitetail bucks is normally effective. However, when more than one buck within a social group develops physically and psychologically to a point where conflict is inevitable, battles over dominance can occur with devastating results. Without the establishment of social order and the dominant–subordinate relationship, the outcome would be devastating to the overall physical and genetic health of the herd.

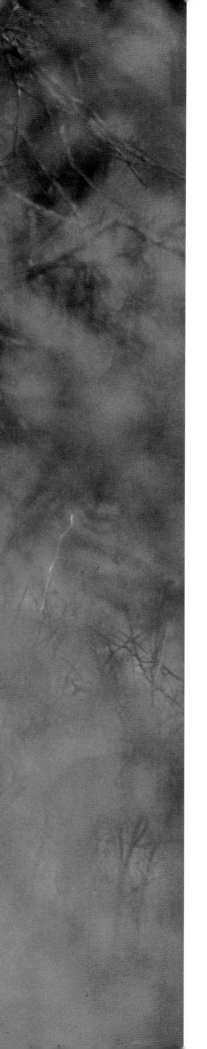

THE NATURE OF THE BEAST

Though whitetails are a docile animal for most of the year, aggression is paramount to the survival of the species. As we have seen, nature provides a highly developed and ordered structure that allows whitetail bucks to work out most of their differences through ritualized dominance displays as well as sparring bouts that occur prior to the onset of the rut. These sparring bouts are initially very mild in intensity, but they gain momentum as the rut approaches. They will eventually lead to more physical encounters of pushing and shoving and occasionally escalate

The sight of a mature whitetail buck can leave an indelible impression on the viewer that may last a lifetime. Even if you have seen a thousand different bucks, you will always remember every detail of the sighting of your biggest buck.

into full-fledged fights. Without the establishment of social order and the dominant–subordinate relationship, the outcome would be devastating to the physical and genetic health of the herd.

Although most mature males live together for the majority of the year in their social fraternities, they will split up and travel independently during the breeding season. As these bucks encounter each other during the rut, subordinates give way to the larger dominant males. Social harmony is maintained, and the resultant

pecking order is seldom in need of reinforcement. Fewer conflicts means less tension and stress, allowing bucks to conserve energy for the daily maintenance functions necessary for survival.

As testosterone levels rise within the buck's bloodstream, his aggression toward other bucks also increases. Mature dominant bucks rarely tolerate the presence of mature subordinate bucks during the breeding season. They will, however, tolerate or ignore yearling or small two-year-olds bucks that may still be living with the

doe family groups. As previously noted, studies have shown that the large dominant males are able to physically and psychologically suppress breeding in these younger males to such an extent that their presence is not a factor.

Nature provides a scheme that allows the genetically superior dominant bucks to lay the groundwork for future generations. Mate selection is a natural byproduct of the process, allowing the dominant males to commingle with dominant females. This framework, however, is dependent upon a healthy sex ratio and age structure within the herd, a dynamic that is missing in many states that promote the harvesting of large numbers of bucks before maturity. Many studies indicate that simply restructuring hunting seasons to bring age and sex ratios into a healthier balance could reduce the negative effects.

Nature's plan is effective in controlling the overly aggressive, dominant nature of males within the herd, but there are times when conflict is unavoidable. Occasionally, more than one buck within a social group develops to the point where a conflict over dominance will occur. Serious battles can erupt from such a conflict, and the results can be devastating for both animals. These battles can leave bucks seriously gored, or exhausted to the point that they are vulnerable to being attacked by opportunistic subordinate bucks or large predators. Death is most likely the reward awaiting a

buck that finds himself in this perilous situation. It is not uncommon for bucks to become locked together in these battles, hopelessly entangled with nothing but doom resulting for both combatants.

A more common scenario, one that unravels every fall, is a dispute or confrontation over an estrous doe. During the rut, dominant bucks roam outside of their normal territories, increasing their range by two to five miles or more. When this occurs, they enter the territories of dominant bucks from other social groups, with whom they have had no previous contact. Without an existing dominant-subordinate relationship to govern their actions, fights are inevitable.

Witnessing one of these confrontations between evenly matched dominant bucks is a breathtaking, thrilling experience that few humans ever observe. Words alone can not illustrate the intensity of a battle between two equally powerful giants. Instances in which these struggles have gone on for hours have been recorded—no doubt leaving the loser and the victor alike in less than satisfactory condition.

When confrontation is inevitable, bucks approach each other like two gladiators. With their necks bowed and their ears laid down and back, they circle each other slowly in a stiff-legged gait. Every hair stands on end, in an effort to dissuade the opponent by inflating body size. They tilt their antlers and turn them side to side in

Words alone are insufficient to describe the intensity of a battle between two equally matched dominant bucks. If initial posturing and bluffing fail to dissuade either combatant, they will lunge together in a violent collision which can break antler tines or whole beams. Nose to nose, bodies low to the ground, their muscles strain and faces contort as each buck pushes and shoves, struggling to gain leverage over his opponent. It is not uncommon for bucks to become locked together in these conflicts, hopelessly entangled with nothing but doom resulting for both.

Leaves, dirt and debris are tossed into the air as each buck labors for an advantage. Vocalizations which may accompany the clashing of antlers attract other bucks hoping to escape with the now unattended doe. Occasionally one buck will flip the opponent onto his back, a position that may prove injurious or even fatal for the unlucky competitor.

an attempt to impress and intimidate the opponent with their formidable appearance. The bucks emit guttural grunts and hissing sounds that one might mistake for air escaping from a flat tire.

Eventually, they make eye contact, and if one or the other fails to back down, they lunge together, clashing antlers in a violent collision that often results in broken tines, or in whole beams snapping from the impact. Nose to nose, antlers entwined, each buck stays low, chest to the ground, pushing and shoving in an attempt to get under the opponent and gain a physical advantage. Muscles strain, faces contort, and necks twist and turn as each buck's legs drive him forward in the effort to gain leverage over his adversary. Grass, leaves, dirt, and other debris sail into the air amidst the flurry of legs struggling for a secure foothold. Grunts, groans, and other vocalizations accompany the clashing of antlers, attracting to the scene other bucks that hope to escape with the now-unattended doe.

Occasionally, one buck gains a physical advantage and flips or hurls the opponent into the air or over onto his back, a position that will most likely prove injurious or even fatal for the unlucky combatant. Inevitably, one buck turns in defeat, tucks his tail, and flees with the victor in hot pursuit, hoping to inflict one final insulting blow to the flank or hindquarter of the defeated rival. The chase is normally short, as the victor

Whitetail Monarchs

Eventually, one buck will turn in defeat, tuck his tail and retreat with the winner in hot pursuit, hoping to deliver one final blow to the hindquarter of the now vanquished foe. The pursuit is normally short lived with the victor not wanting to venture far from the doe that has been won from the conflict.

does not want to venture far from the doe that has been won as a result of the conflict.

So it is with the whitetail buck. The winner assumes the position as master of his domain; the loser, if he survives, is relegated to a subordinate position. Aggression, dominance, and survival of the fittest all combine to determine a victor—one superior animal, one buck to serve as the alpha male. This is probably a different scenario than the one many people associate with the whitetail, but it is a reality nonetheless.

To the casual observer, it would seem unthinkable as we enter the twenty-first century that the massive herds in existence today are anything but a healthy resource that will thrive into the twenty-second century and beyond. Yet we must remember that our ancestors applied this same thinking to the herds that existed in the mid-1800s. Many outdoorsmen, researchers, and biologists are raising serious questions concerning the current management strategies for this species. Many feel that our herds nationwide have peaked, and that serious problems may lie on the horizon for

this magnificent animal unless management of whitetails enters a new era. Many would argue that restocking efforts and the goal of returning the whitetail to all the available range that it once occupied has been accomplished. With this goal met, they argue, efforts should now be directed at improving the health and quality of the herd rather than concentrating on pure numbers alone.

If the overall health of the nation's whitetail herd is to be measured by appropriate sex and age ratios, as well as by numbers that conform to the carrying capacity of available habitat, then many states are faced with a major dilemma. Development of management strategies that would establish healthier buck-to-doe ratios and age structures may be the greatest challenge facing the researchers, biologists, and game managers who control the majority of our deer herds nationwide. Addressing these problems now will assure healthy herds for generations to come.

We must always remember that the whitetail deer is an extremely adaptable species, a prolific breeder capable of producing numbers that far exceed the carrying capacity of our lands as they exist today. We must understand that the successful restoration of the whitetail to its present numbers has brought with it substantial problems, such as decreased habitat and competition for available resources, that did not exist centuries ago. We must not forget

that the role of management of the whitetail and most other big game species is no longer in the hands of the four-legged predators that co-existed with the whitetail populations during the pre-Columbian era. That role has fallen on the shoulders of humans, many of whom have been more influenced by animated cartoon characters, folklore, and myth than by biological fact.

An understanding of the needs of the animal, as well as the needs of the people who for various reasons pursue or manage the whitetail, is paramount to a continued, successful future for the species. Attitudes toward buck-only management and harvest strategies must change, as they have in several states around the nation. The belief that "they can't grow big if they don't grow old" has finally taken root in some hunting camps around the nation. Many states have instituted game laws that limit the harvest of yearling bucks and place an emphasis on reducing the doe population while allowing more bucks to reach a higher level of maturity. Without these laws and the accompanying human values that must exist, the chances of seeing one of these great animals in the wild will be severely diminished.

A preponderance of data exists indicating that reducing herd size below the maximum carrying capacity of the land creates greater opportunity for each animal within the herd to develop to its maximum potential. Herd stress as a result of overcrowding is minimized, increasing reproduction

The Nature of the Beast

rates, improving the physical development of younger deer, and lowering the rates of mortality due to poor nutrition. However, we do not yet know whether all states will respond positively to this research and set a new course for their herds in the twenty-first century. Attempts to modify our herds and create a healthier balance will, of course, be met with great human resistance. The old beliefs among many whitetail enthusiasts concerning the management of the species are difficult if not impossible to change.

One organization committed to this mission has evolved in the past decade and may eventually have a positive effect on changing many of our views concerning whitetail management and hunting practices. The Quality Deer Management Association is dedicated to "extending the hunter's role from a mere consumer to a manager. Quality Deer Management (QDM), in part, is the use of restraint in harvesting young bucks combined with an adequate harvest of female deer to maintain a healthy herd." This conservation-minded organization "promotes hunter ethics,

sound deer management, and better relationships among landowners, hunters, non-hunters, and biologists through education." This process must continue if our herds are to prosper over the next one hundred years.

The role of the hunter in many of our successful conservation efforts should not be overlooked. The Pittman-Robertson Act (The Federal Aid in Wildlife Restoration Act of 1937), which placed taxes on equipment purchased by sportsmen, has generated well over three billion dollars since its inception. These funds have been directed toward the restoration of many valuable wildlife species, including the whitetail deer. Nationwide, hunters comprise only about eight percent of our population, but the monies they spend on hunting licenses alone provide as much as seventy-five percent of the funds available for state wildlife conservation programs aimed at both game and non-game species. Although hunting is viewed and classified as a consumptive sport, its effect on all wildlife when conducted in an ethical manner must be viewed as positive.

Recently, I returned to the small North Texas town I wrote about in the beginning of this book. The visit, of course, brought back many memories from my youth—most notably my first excursions into the outdoors with my father, as well as my first contact with a whitetail deer. I was pleasantly surprised to find the whitetail abundant and thriving in the surrounding countryside. During an evening drive, a large bachelor group crossed the road directly in front of my truck. The largest member of the group, a respectable ten-point buck, paused by the side of the road as I pulled to a stop. It was as if my search for the elusive giant I dreamed of seeing as a child nearly forty years earlier had finally come full circle.

I considered the many years I had waited as a young man to come face to face with one of these great kings of the autumn woods, and thought about what a sad situation it would be if my children or their children could never experience the thrill I had experienced in the Hagerman Refuge more than a decade earlier. Hopefully, the future of the whitetail deer in North America will remain bright, and the opportunity to see and admire whitetail monarchs will exist for all who enter the autumn woods.

The Nature of the Beast

As we enter the 21st Century we must not forget that the successful future of the whitetail deer is dependent upon proper education of the general public who must gain an understanding of the biological, social and environmental needs of the whitetail. They must learn not be influenced by animated cartoon characters, folklore and myth.

We must always remember:
The whitetail deer is a prolific breeder and an
extremely adaptable creature.

We must understand:
Successful restoration of the whitetail to its present
day numbers has brought with it substantial
problems not in existence centuries ago.

We must not forget:
Management of the whitetail is no longer in the hands
of predators that coexisted with the whitetail in times gone by.
That role has fallen upon the shoulders of humans.

SELECTED REFERENCES

Atkeson, T. D. and R. L. Marchinton. 1982. Forehead glands in white-tailed deer. *J. Mammal.* 63:613-617.

Atkeson, T. D., V. F. Nettles, R. L. Marchinton and W. V. Branan. 1988. Nasal glands in the Cervidae. *J. Mammal.* 69:153-156.

Banks, W. J. 1974. The ossification process of the developing antler in the white-tailed deer (*Odocoileus virginianus*). *Calc. Tissue Res.* 14:257-274.

Benner J. M. and R. T. Bowyer, 1988. Selection of trees for rubs by white-tailed deer in Maine. *J. Mammal.* 69:624-627.

Blackard, J.J. 1971. Restoration of the white-tailed deer in the Southeastern United States. M.S. Thesis, Louisiana State Univ., Baton Rouge, LA 171 pp.

Brothers, A., and M. E. Ray, Jr. 1975. *Producing quality white-tails.* Caesar Kleberg Wildlife Research Institute, Kingsville, TX. 246 pp.

Brown, R. D., ed. 1983. *Antler Development in Cervidae.* Caesar Kleberg Wildlife Research Institute, Kingsville, TX. 480 pp.

Bubenik, G. A., and A. B. Bubenik. 1986. *Phylogenic and onto-genic development of antlers and neuroendocrine regulation of the antler cycle—a review.* Saugetierkudl. Mitt. 33:97-123.

Bubenik, G. A., and A. B. Bubenik, eds. 1990. *Horns, prong-horns, and antlers: evolution, morphology, physiology, and social significance.* Springer-Verlag New York Inc., 562 pp.

Cox, D. J., and J. J. Ozoga. 1988. *Whitetail Country.* Willow Creek Press, Minocqua, WI 145 pp.

Dasman, W. 1971. *If deer are to survive.* Stackpole Books. Harrisburg, PA. 129 pp.

Decker, D. J. and N. A. Connelly. 1990. The need for hunter education in deer management: insights from New York. *Wildl. Soc. Bull.* 18:447-452.

De Vos, A. 1967. Rubbing of conifers by white-tailed deer in successive years. *J. Mammal* 48:146-147.

Follman, E. H., and W. D. Kilmstra. 1969. Fertility in male white-tailed deer fawns. *Journal of Wildlife Management.* 33:708-711.

Forand, K. J., R. L. Marchinton, and K. V. Miller. 1989. Influence of dominance rank on the antler cycle of white-tailed deer. *J. Mammal.* 66:58-62.

Geist V. 1995. Mule deer and white-tailed deer beginnings. *Deer & Deer Hunting* 18(5): 66-71.

Geist V. and F. Walther, eds. 1974. *The behavior of ungulates and its relation to management,* 1 vol. New Series Publ. 24. Morges, Switzerland: IUCN. 940 pp.

Gerlach, D., S. Atwater, and J. Schnell (Eds.). 1994. *Deer.* Stackpole Books. Mechanicsburg, PA 384 pp.

Goss, R.J. 1983. *Deer antlers: regeneration, function, and evolution.* Academic Press, NY. 316 pp.

Goss, R.J. 1969. Photoperiodic control of antler cycles in deer: I. Phase shift and frequency changes. *J. Exp. Zool.* 170 (3):311-324.

Halls, L. K., ed. 1984. *White-tailed deer: ecology and management.* Wildlife Managemen. Institute, The Stackpole Co., Harrisburg, PA. 870 pp.

Hawkins, R. E., and W. D. Klimstra. 1970. A preliminary study of social organization of white-tailed deer. *J. Wildlife Mgmt.* 34: 407-419.

Hirth, D. H. 1977. Observations of loss of antler velvet in white-tailed deer. *Southwestern Naturalist* 22:269-286.

Hirth, D. H. 1977. *Social behavior of white-tailed deer in relation to habitat.* Wildl. Monogr. 53. 55 pp.

Hirth D. H. 1985. Mother-young behavior in white-tailed deer. *Odocoileus virginianus. Southwestern Naturalist* 30:297-302.

Holzenbein, S., and R. L. Marchinton. 1992. Spatial integration of maturing-male white-tailed deer into the adult popula-tion. *J. Mammal* 73:326-334.

Holzenbein S., and G. Schwede. 1989. Activity and movements of female white-tailed deer during the rut. *J. Wildl. Manage.* 53:219-223.

Jefferies, L. 1975. *Deer stocking program in Georgia 1928-1974.* Georgia Dep. Nat. Resour., Fed. Aid Wildl. Restor. 39 pp.

Johnson, A. S., P.E., Hale, J. M. Wentworth, and J. S. Osborne. 1986. Are we really managing deer populations? Annu. Meet. Southeast Deer Study Group 9:9-10.

Kay, R.N.B., M. Phillippo, J. M. Suttie, and G. Wenham. 1981. The growth and mineralization of antlers. *J. Physiol.* 322:4P.

Kile. T. L., and R. L. Marchinton. 1977. White-tailed deer rubs and scrapes: spatial, temporal and physical characteristics and social role. *Am. Midl. Nat.* 97:257-266.

Magruder, N. D., C. E. French, L.C. McEwen, and R. W. Swift. 1957. Nutritional requirements of white-tailed deer for growth and antler development II. Pennsylvania State Agric. Exp. Stn. Bull. 628. 21 pp.

Marchinton, R. L., J. R. Fudge, J. C. Fortson, K. V. Miller, and D. A. Dobie. 1991. Genetic stock and environment as factors in production of record class antlers. Pages 315-318 in B. Bobek, K. Perzanowski, and W. L. Regelin, eds. *Global trends in wildlife management*. Vol. 1. Trans. 18th Congr. Int. Union Game Biol. 1987. Swiat Press, Krakow-Warszawa.

Marchinton, R. L., K. L. Johansen and K. V. Miller. 1990. Behavioral components of white-tailed deer scent marking; social and seasonal effects. Pages 295-301 in D. W. Mac Donald, D. Muller-Schwarze, and S. E. Matynczuk, eds. *Chemical signals in Vertebrates* 5. Oxford Univ. Press.

Marchinton, R. L., K. V. Miller, R. J. Hamilton and D. C. Guynn. 1990. Quality deer management: biological and social impacts on the herd. Pages 7-15 in C. Kyser, D. C. Sisson and J. L. Landers, eds. *Proc. Tall Timbers Game Bird Seminar, Tallahassee, Fla.*

Marchinton, R. L., R. J. Hamilton, K. V. Miller, E. L. Marchinton, T. L. Kile and W. Cooper. 1993. Quality deer management: A paradigm for the future? *Quality Whitetails* 1:6-9.

McCabe, Richard and McCabe, Thomas 1984. Of slings and arrows: an historical retrospection. Pages 16-72 in L.K. Halls, ed. *White-tailed deer: ecology and management*. Stackpole Books, Harrisburg, PA. 870 pp.

McCullough, D. R. 1979. *The George Reserve deer herd:* population ecology of a K-selected species. Ann Arbor: Univ. Michigan Press. 271 pp.

McCullough D. R., D. H. Hirth, and S. J. Newhouse. 1989. Resource partitioning between the sexes in white-tailed deer. *J. Wildl. Manage.* 53:277-283.

McDonald, S., and K. V. Miller. 1994. Reconstruction: How the South's deer herds were rebuilt. *Deer & Deer Hunting* 17(6):26-32.

Michael, E. D. 1964. Birth of white-tailed deer fawns. *J. Wildlife Mgmt.* 28: 171-173.

Miller, K. V., R. L. Marchinston and W. M. Knox. 1991. White-tailed deer signposts and their role as a source of priming pheromones: a hypothesis. Pages 455-458 in B. Bobek, K. Perzanowski, and W. Regelin, eds. *Global trends in wildlife management*. Trans. 18th IUGB Congress, Krakow 1987. Swiat Press, Krakow-Warszawa.

Miller, K. V., and R. L. Marchinton eds. 1995. *Quality whitetails: the why and how of quality deer management*. Stackpole Books, PA 322 pp.

Miller, K. V., K. E. Kammermeyer, R. L. Marchinton and B. Moser. 1987. Population and habitat influences on antler rubbing by white-tailed deer. *J. Wildl. Manage.* 51:62-66.

Miller, K. V., Rl. L. Marchinton, K. J. Forand and K. L. Johansen. 1987. Dominance, testosterone levels, and scraping activity in a captive herd of white-tailed deer. *J. Mammal* 68:812-817.

Miller, K. V., O. E. Rhodes, Jr., T. R. Litchfield, M. H. Smith and R. L. Marchinton, 1987. Reproductive characteristics of yearling and adult male white-tailed deer. Proc. Annu. Conf. Southeast Assoc. Fish and Wildl. Agencies 41:378-384.

Miller K. V., R. L. Marchinton, J. R. Beckwith, and P. B. Bush. 1985. Variations in density and chemical composition of white-tailed deer antlers. *J. Mammal.* 66:693-701.

Nelson, M.E., and L. D. Mech. 1992. Dispersal in female white-tailed deer. *J. Mammal.* 73: 891-894.

Nelson, M.E., and L. D. Mech. 1984. Home-range formation and dispersal of deer in Northeastern Minnesota. *J. Mammal* 65:567-575.

Nelson, M. E. and L. D. Mech. 1990. Weights, productivity, and mortality of old white-tailed deer. *J. Mammal.* 17:689-691.

Nelsen, D. G., M. J. Dunlap and K. V. Miller. 1982. Pre-rut rubbing by white-tailed bucks: nursery damage, social role, and management options. *Wildl. Soc. Bull.* 10:341-348.

Nesbitt, W. H., and P. L. Wright. 1985. *Measuring and scoring North American big game trophies*. Boone and Crockett Club. Missoula, Mont. 176 pp.

Ozoga, J. J. 1972. Aggressive behavior of white-tailed deer at winter cuttings. *J. Wildl. Manage.* 36:892-896.

Ozoga, J. J. 1988. Incidence of "infant" antlers among supplementally fed white-tailed deer. *J. Mammal* 69:393-395.

Ozoga, J. J. 1994. Competitive signposting. *Deer & Deer Hunting* 17(7):46-47.

Ozoga, J. J. 1994. The overhead limb—for bucks only. *Deer & Deer Hunting.*

Ozoga, J. J. 1994. *Whitetail Autumn: seasons of the whitetail. Book One.* Willow Creek Press., Minocqua, Wisconsin. 160 pp.

Ozoga, J. J. 1996. *Whitetail Spring. Whitetail autumn: seasons of the whitetail. Book Three.* Willow Creek Press., Minocqua, Wisconsin. 144 pp.

Ozoga, J. J. 1997. *Whitetail Summer. Whitetail autumn: seasons of the whitetail. Book Four.* Willow Creek Press., Minocqua, Wisconsin. 144 pp.

Ozoga, J. J. 1995. *Whitetail Winter. Whitetail autumn: seasons of the whitetail. Book Two.* Willow Creek Press., Minocqua, Wisconsin. 160 pp.

Ozoga, J. J. and L. W. Gysel. 1972. Response of white-tailed deer to winter weather. *J. Wildl. Manage.* 36:892-896.

Ozoga, J. J., and L. J. Verme. 1975. Activity patterns of white-tailed deer during estrus. *J. Wildl. Manage.* 39:679-683.

Ozoga, J. J., and L. J. Verme. 1985. Comparative breeding behavior and performance of yearling vs. prime-age white-tailed bucks. *J. Wildl. Manage.* 49:364-372.

Ozoga, J. J, and L. J. Verme. 1986. Relation of maternal age to fawn-rearing success in white-tailed deer. *J. Wildlife Mgmt.* 50: 480-486.

Peterle. T. J. 1975. Deer sociobiology. *Wildl. Soc. Bull* 3:82-83.

Pielou, E. C. 1991. *After the Ice Age:* the return of life to glaciated North America. The University of Chicago Press, Chicago, IL. 366 pp.

Reneau, Jack and Reneau, Susan, *Records of North American Whitetail Deer.* 3rd Edition, Boone and Crockett Club, Missoula, MT. 432 pp.

Robinson, W. L. 1962. Social dominance and physical condition among penned white-tailed deer fawns. *J. Mammal.* 43:462-469.

Rongstad. O. J., and J. R. Tester. 1969. Movements and habitat use of white-tailed deer. *J. Wildl. Manage.* 33:366-379.

Rue. L. L. III. 1989. *The Deer of North America.* 2nd edition, updated and expanded. Outdoor Life Books. Grolier Book Club Inc., Danbury, CT 508 pp.

Sawyer, T. G., R. L. Marchinton and K. V. Miller. 1989. Response of female white-tailed deer to scrapes and antler rubs. *J. Mammal.* 70:431-433.

Schwede, G., H. Hendrichs, and C. Wemmer. 1994. Early mother-young relations in white-tailed deer. *J. Mammal.* 75:438-445.

Schultz, S. R. and M. K. Johnson. 1992. Chronology of antler velvet shedding in captive Louisiana white-tailed deer. *J. Wildl. Mgmt.* 56:651-655.

Shea, S. M., T. A. Brault, and M. L. Richardson. 1992. Herd density and physical condition of white-tailed deer in Florida flatwoods. *J. Wildl. Mgmt.* 56:262-267.

Townsend, T. W., and E. D. Bailey. 1981. Effects of age, sex and weight on social rank in penned white-tailed deer. *Am. Midl. Nat.* 106:92-101.

Verme. L. J. 1965. Reproduction studies on penned white-tailed deer. *J. Wildl. Manage.* 29:74-79.

Verme. L. J. 1962. Mortality of white-tailed deer fawns. Proc. Nat. White-tailed Deer Dis. Symp. 1: 15-38.

Verme L. J. 1963. Effect of nutrition on growth of white-tailed deer fawns. Trans. N. Amer. Wildl. and Natur. Resour. Conf. 28: 431-443.

Verme. L. J. 1983. Sex ratio variations in *Odocoileus:* a critical review. *J. Wildlife Mgmt.* 47:573-582.

Verme. L. J. and R. V. Doepker. 1988. Suppression of reproduction in Upper Michigan white-tailed deer. *Odocoileus virginianus,* by climatic stress during the rut. *Canadian Field Nat.* 102:550-552.

Verme, L. J. and J. J. Ozoga. 1971 Influence of winter weather on white-tailed deer in Upper Michigan. Page 16-28 in A. O. Haugen, ed. Proc. Snow and Ice Symposium, Iowa State Univ.

Verme. L. J. and J. J. Ozoga. 1980. Effects of diet on growth and lipogenesis in deer fawns. *J. Wildl. Manage.* 44:315-324.

Whitney, M. D., D. L. Forester, K. V. Miller and R. L. Marchinton. 1991. Sexual attraction in white-tailed deer. Pages 327-333 in R. D. Brown, ed. *The biology of deer.* Springer-Verlag.

Whittington, G. July 1992. Seminar: Deer Management and Trophy Hunting. Dallas, Texas.

Woods, G. R., R. J. Hamilton, D. C. Guynn, R. L. Marchinton and K. V. Miller. 1993. How whitetails use traditional rubs. *Deer & Deer Hunting* 17(4)30-36.